Bond  EDITION

11$^+$ Test Papers

Maths

Multiple-choice

The secrets of 11$^+$ success

Text © Andrew Baines 2007
Original illustrations © Nelson Thornes Ltd 2007

The right of Andrew Baines to be identified as author of this work has been asserted by him in accordance with the Copyright, Designs and Patents Act 1988.

All rights reserved. No part of this publication may be reproduced or transmitted in any form or by any means, electronic or mechanical, including photocopying, recording or any information storage and retrieval system, without permission in writing from the publisher or under licence from the Copyright Licensing Agency Ltd, of Saffron House, 6–10 Kirby Street, London, EC1N 8TS.

Any person who commits any unauthorised act in relation to this publication may be liable to criminal prosecution and civil claims for damages.

First published in 2003 by:
Nelson Thornes Ltd

This edition published in 2007 by:
Nelson Thornes Ltd, Delta Place, 27 Bath Road
CHELTENHAM GL53 7TH, United Kingdom

07 08 09 10 11 / 10 9 8 7 6 5 4 3 2 1

A catalogue record for this book is available from the British Library

ISBN 978 0 7487 8482 0

Page make-up by Tech Set Ltd

Printed and bound in Croatia by Zrinski

Published by Nelson Thornes. Nelson Thornes is a Wolters Kluwer company, and is not associated in any way with NFER-Nelson.

Nelson Thornes
a Wolters Kluwer business

The secrets of 11+ success in maths

How 11+ exams work

Approaching 11+ exams for the first time can be a daunting experience. They are unlike any other school exam your child will take for several reasons:

- *There's no pass mark.* Success or failure depends on your child's performance relative to the performance of other children sitting the test. The pass mark can vary from year to year and from school to school.

- *They can't be retaken.* There is no second chance with the 11+ so it all rests on your child's performance on the day.

- *There's no national syllabus.* 11+ exams vary from area to area, and often from town to town. Often schools are extremely unwilling to give out any information about the content of the exams.

- *It's often impossible to see past papers.* This varies from area to area but the actual papers usually remain a closely guarded secret.

- *Selective schools give out very little advice.* It is common for selective schools to give out only the vaguest advice to parents when approaching the exam and to discourage very much practice.

All these factors make preparing a child for the 11+ a mysterious and often stressful process for parent and child alike. The most common question parents ask about using practice tests is 'What percentage does my child need to get to pass?' Unfortunately there's no easy answer to this but we can give guidance. (See 'What a score means and how to boost it' on page 3.) The second most common question is 'How can I help them improve?' The following sections give our tutors' top tips to help your child through the 11+ process and boost their scores. We strongly recommend that you think about purchasing at least two of the Bond books mentioned inside the front cover. These are:

- *The Parents' Stress-free Guide to the 11+.* The essential manual that provides a simple and practical 4-Step system for making the most of 11+ preparation.

- *How to do … 11+ Maths.* All the question types in these tests are fully explained in this guide to 11+ maths.

Tutors' top tips for 11+ success

- *Find out what exams your child will sit but don't agonise over 'school gate gossip'.* Find out what the exams are and get the advice that the secondary schools give out, but don't waste your energy following rumours about what the pass mark is or exactly which questions will come up. It's better to spend your time helping your child.

- *It's always worth practising.* Whatever secondary schools say, it's worth it. Children can improve their performance by 10–15 per cent by careful practice.

- *Start early if you can, but don't worry if you haven't.* Ideally it is best to start preparation for the 11+ exam at least one year ahead. However, don't panic if you don't have that much time – even a few weeks can make a difference.

- *Make a simple action plan.* However long you've got, have a clear, simple strategy. There are two key principles:
  - start from your child's present level of knowledge
  - help your child to learn from their mistakes.

The Parents' Stress-free Guide to the 11+ provides a set of ready-made action plans you can use, whether you have two years or just a few weeks to go.

- *Motivation, motivation, motivation!* You have to take your child with you on this journey. A simple rewards system can be highly effective. *The Parents' Stress-free Guide to the 11+* can provide a tried and tested motivational system if you want one.

- *Don't just practise.* There's a tendency to think that just practising one paper after another will do the trick. It's far more important to learn from mistakes. Going through the paper afterwards with your child and filling in the gaps in learning is crucial.

- *Stay calm, manage stress, build confidence.* Don't talk about the 11+ all the time. Use breaks, treats and bite-sized learning sessions to keep things fresh. Be realistic about your child's potential. Pass or fail, it's important to try to make this process a positive one.

- *Manage the exam day.* Make sure that you have everything ready for the day, that your child tries to get a good night's sleep, eats breakfast and gets there in good time.

How and when to use these tests

- *It's best to use them as real exam practice.* These tests are mock exams. They are set out in a style as close as possible to the real thing – though the format will vary from area to area. It is best to use them as authentic exam experience rather than for general practice, and to use them quite close to the exam. Follow the instructions in the answers booklet on timings and administering the tests.

What a score means and how to boost it

For the reasons given above, it is impossible to say that a certain score can guarantee a pass in the actual exams. However, we suggest that a score of 85% (42/50) would be a standard to aim at, without using this as a benchmark to frighten your child with. The best motivator is to see the scores going up. Here are some tried and tested tips for improvement:

- *Go over any incorrect answers.* Always go over incorrect answers so that your child can see what went wrong. To help with this process, each answer in these test papers is explained and also has an individual tutorial reference icon: [B1]. This icon links to the relevant section in *How to do … 11⁺ Maths* so your child can read more about the related topic and complete more practice questions if needed.

- *Use the Next Steps Planner inside the front cover.* This will provide a plan for what to do next when a test has been marked.

- *Improve basic exam technique.* Work on improving speed, working efficiently – coming back to trickier questions later – and pacing over the 50 minutes.

- *Improve basic maths.* Ensure the foundations are strong enough. Use the checklist in the section below to help.

- *Avoid the two most common maths errors.* These are:
  - not reading the question correctly
  - making a silly error in a question you know perfectly well how to answer.

Identify the 'silly mistakes' with your child. Get them to ring these mistakes themselves in pen so that they really see them.

- *Target what you don't know* – the secret is not to keep blindly practising but relentlessly to target the maths your child doesn't know. This is where crucial marks can be picked up.

The maths you need for 11⁺ exams

Unlike reasoning exams, for which your child has to practise special skills, maths for 11⁺ is just a continuation of the work your child does every day at school. Some of the questions may be a little harder, but they test the same skills and content.

11⁺ maths will draw on a number of key areas in line with the National Curriculum and the national numeracy strategy. These can be broken down into a number of sub-topics as follows:

All these areas will be covered in these papers, but your child may be weaker on some than others. The tutors' answer explanations will help your child see how each question should be solved. For more detailed explanations of strategies and further practice of particular sub-topics, follow the tutorial links to the relevant sections in *How to do ... 11⁺ Maths.*

Number	Fractions and decimals	Handling data	Shape and space	Measurement
1 Place value 2 Addition and subtraction problems 3 Multiplication and division problems 4 Mixed or several-step problems 5 Factors and multiples 6 Special numbers 7 Sequences 8 Equations and algebra 9 Function machines	10 Fractions 11 Decimal fractions 12 Percentages 13 Ratio and proportion	14 Organising and comparing information 15 Mean, median, mode and range 16 Probability	17 2D shapes: circles, angles and bearings 18 2D shapes: triangles 19 2D shapes: quadrilaterals and polygons 20 Perimeter and area 21 3D shapes 22 Volume and capacity 23 Transformations 24 Symmetry	25 Metric and imperial measures 26 Reading scales 27 Time and timetables

Basic skills checklist

All maths topics are underpinned by a set of basic skills. We suggest that it is worthwhile reinforcing these if your child is having problems. As follows:

1 Check number bonds to twenty. Can they easily add and subtract numbers with answers up to 20?

2 Support times tables facts. For the purposes of 11⁺ maths it is crucial that children are fluent in their tables up to 12 × 12.

3 Help your child with place value. Can they read whole numbers to a million and multiply or divide any whole number by 10 quickly?

4 Help your child with doubling and halving. Your child should be able to double all numbers to 50 and half all numbers to 100 quickly.

5 Revise the four number operations: + − × ÷.

6 Check units of measurement. Both metric and imperial for key lengths, weights and capacities.

For more details on how to support these basic skills, see *How to do ... 11⁺ Maths* pages 1-6.

Bond NEW EDITION

11⁺ Test Papers

Maths

Multiple-choice – Notes / Answers

This booklet contains:

- advice on how to administer the tests

- answers

- tutors' explanations for every answer

- links to *How to do … 11⁺ Maths*

Text © Andrew Baines 2007
Original illustrations © Nelson Thornes Ltd 2007

The right of Andrew Baines to be identified as author of this work has been asserted by him in accordance with the Copyright, Designs and Patents Act 1988.

All rights reserved. No part of this publication may be reproduced or transmitted in any form or by any means, electronic or mechanical, including photocopying, recording or any information storage and retrieval system, without permission in writing from the publisher or under licence from the Copyright Licensing Agency Ltd, of Saffron House, 6–10 Kirby Street, London, EC1N 8TS.

Any person who commits any unauthorised act in relation to this publication may be liable to criminal prosecution and civil claims for damages.

First published in 2003 by:
Nelson Thornes Ltd

This edition published in 2007 by:
Nelson Thornes Ltd, Delta Place, 27 Bath Road, CHELTENHAM GL53 7TH, UK
07 08 09 10 11 / 10 9 8 7 6 5 4 3 2 1
A catalogue record for this book is available from the British Library

ISBN 978 0 7487 8482 0

Page make-up by Tech Set Ltd

Printed and bound in Croatia by Zrinski

Published by Nelson Thornes. Nelson Thornes is a Wolters Kluwer company, and is not associated in any way with NFER-Nelson.

How to administer the tests

What do you need?

- A quiet, well-lit place to sit the test.
- A stock of pencils.
- A pencil sharpener and an eraser.
- Blank paper for rough working.
- A clock or timer.
- *Calculators are not allowed.*

Before you start

Try to provide a calm yet formal atmosphere in which your child can take the test. It is important that you re-create the real test as closely as possible, so try to ensure your child has an appropriate work space and no distractions. Choose a time to do a test when your child is rested and relaxed.

Multiple-choice tests ask children to mark their answers in a separate answer booklet. Therefore, when reading the front page of the test paper with your child, point out the importance of answering carefully and rubbing out any altered answers clearly. (Read the section below for details of common pitfalls that can occur when using multiple-choice answer booklets.) Ensure that enough rough paper is available for working out answers; they should not use the empty space on the paper for workings.

Allow 50 minutes per test. On average, they will have one minute to answer each question, so encourage them to move on from questions they are stuck on before too much time is wasted. Your child may find it helpful to put a cross in pencil by questions that have been missed out so that they can be quickly spotted later on. Remind them that they can always go back at the end if they have time left. Finish reading the instructions together before you 'start the clock'.

When the time is up they should stop writing. If they have not finished, draw a line at the point they have reached. You can always allow them to continue after the time to get more practice, or else leave the other questions blank for another day. Encourage them to think about whether they should try to speed up, or to work more carefully, depending on how they finish the paper.

Using the multiple-choice answer booklet

If your child is sitting a multiple-choice exam it is crucial that they understand how to use the answer booklet properly. Spend time examining the booklet together. As you look through it explain that multiple-choice answer sheets are usually scored by computer rather than by hand, (an optical reader scans the marks on each page). As a result, an answer will be classed as wrong if it is not clearly and accurately marked.

There are some common mistakes that are easy to make when using a multiple-choice answer booklet. Talk through the following points carefully with your child, without panicking them, but so that they understand exactly what they should / should not do:

- *Marking outside the box.* To record an answer, a clear line should be made through the centre of the relevant answer box. The line should stay within the border of the box so that it can be read accurately by the computer.

- *Crossing out an answer.* If your child wants to change their mind they must never cross out an answer in a multiple-choice booklet. It must be fully rubbed out and then the new answer should be clearly marked in the appropriate box. If any mark is left in the first box, the computer could read two answers for that question and mark their response as incorrect.

- *Marking an answer in the wrong grid.* Answer grids often look the same on multiple-choice answer sheets so it is easy to mark an answer in the wrong grid, which can have a knock-on effect for all successive answers. Encourage your child to check that the question number of the grid matches the question they are answering before they make each mark. They should also take extra care if they decide to miss out a question to return to later.

- *Not pressing hard enough.* If a mark is too light, it may not be recognised by the computer and the question could be marked wrong. Remind your child that each answer needs to be marked clearly. We would suggest practising with soft HB pencils as they tend to make the clearest marks. If your child has to provide their own pencils for the actual test, make sure they take one or two HB pencils with them.

Marking and feedback

The answers that follow should be given one mark unless otherwise indicated. Do not take marks away for wrong answers, but do not award half marks. You will end up with a score out of 50. Double the score to get a percentage out of 100. 42/50 equals the target score of 85% (see 'The secrets of 11⁺ success in maths' booklet).

After marking, follow these steps:

- *Go over any incorrect answers.* Always go over incorrect answers so that your child can see what went wrong. To help with this process, each answer in these test papers is explained and also has an individual tutorial reference icon: B1 . This icon links to the relevant section in *How to do … 11⁺ Maths* so your child can read more about the related topic and complete more practice questions if needed.

- *Use the Next Steps Planner inside the front cover.* This will provide a plan for what to do next when a test has been marked.

Question number	Answer		📖
1	E	All the angles in this shape are right angles. The other shapes each have two obtuse angles.	B19
2	D	Each child pays £$(x + y)$, 45 children pay $45 \times (x + y)$.	B8
3	B	$3x - 7 = 5$ (subtract $3x$ from both sides) $\quad 3x = 12$ (add 7 to both sides) $\quad\quad x = 4$ (divide both sides by 3)	B8
4	E	From the graph, 20 kg is approximately 44 lb. Multiply both values by 10 to get: 200 kg is approximately 440 lb.	B14
5	D	The 'T' shape is a classic net of a cuboid. You can cut out this shape and fold it to form a 3-D box without any of the sides overlapping and without there being any sides missing.	B21
6	R	Shape R has 6 vertices (corners) and 5 faces.	B21
7	C	$(3 \times £4.75) + (7 \times £3.20) + (12 \times £2) = £14.25 + £22.40 + £24 = £60.65$	B4
8	A	Each small division on this scale represents 0.02. The arrow is one small division past 7.6 so the number it is pointing to is $7.6 + 0.02 = 7.62$.	B6
9	C	$790 \div 5 = 158$	B3
10	B	$5^4 = 5 \times 5 \times 5 \times 5$	B6
11	D	$125 \times £3.99$ (Or round £3.99 up to £4 and then use $125 \times £4 = £500$. Rounding £3.99 to £4 added 1p so we need to subtract $125 \times 1p = £1.25$ from the total. $£500 - £1.25 = £498.75$)	B3
12	A	$100 - 82 = 18$ (the total number of children minus the sum of all the cells shown in the table)	B14
13	C	The third decimal place is 4, so the number rounds down.	B1
14	B	$35 \text{ km} = 35 \times 1000 \text{ m} = 35\,000 \times 100 \text{ cm} = 3\,500\,000 \text{ cm}$ $3\,500\,000 \div 175\,000 = 20 \text{ cm}$ (Or use ratios: 1 cm : 175 000 cm = 1 cm : 1.75 km so 10 cm : 17.5 km so 20 cm : 35 km.)	B3
15	D	Convert the options into decimals, to 3 decimal places: $\frac{4}{7} = 0.571\ldots \quad\quad \frac{7}{12} = 0.583\ldots \quad\quad \frac{4}{6} = \frac{2}{3} = 0.666\ldots \quad\quad \frac{9}{16} = 0.5625 \quad\quad \frac{5}{8} = 0.625$ (Note that each of the fractions B–E is the first fraction after $\frac{1}{2}$ for its denominator ($\frac{7}{12} = \frac{6}{12} + \frac{1}{12}$, $\frac{4}{6} = \frac{3}{6} + \frac{1}{6}$, etc.). This means that the fraction with the largest denominator will have the value closest to $\frac{1}{2}$ (it will have the smallest number added to $\frac{1}{2}$). This will be the smallest number of the numbers B–E and can then be compared with A by converting both numbers to decimals.)	B11
16	B	D and E contain numbers that aren't primes. The cube numbers are 1, 8, 27, ...	B6
17	E	The Harbour Master is 4 units to the right, 6.5 units up.	B23
18	A	The difference between sequential numbers is 11, going up or going across. (Or use the diagonal symmetry of the numbers.)	B7
19	A	Starting from the top left, add up the length of the sides. $11 + 9 + 7 + 3 + (11 - 7) + (9 - 3) = 40 \text{ m}$ (Or use the perimeter of the equivalent rectangle $= (2 \times 11) + (2 \times 9) = 40 \text{ m.}$)	B20
20	D	$57 \div 11 = 5$ remainder 2 so 6 trips are needed to take all the pupils.	B4
21	B	The median is the middle number when the numbers are placed in order of value.	B15
22	B	When rotated, this is the only shape that looks exactly the same as it did in its original position.	B24
23	E	Area of outer rectangle − Area of corner rectangle $= (8 \times 7) - (2 \times 3) = 50 \text{ m}^2$	B20
24	C	Forward 3 (therefore not B or E), second turn is left (therefore not D), then forward 4 (therefore not A).	B17
25	C	The final shape has 4 sides (so not D) with no right angles (so not A or B) and two lines of symmetry (so not E).	B19
26	D	Reverse the calculation: $(142 - 4) \div 3 = 46$	B9

3

Question number	Answer		
27	C	Most standard juice cartons hold 1 litre. A small plastic bag from a supermarket will hold 3.5 litres. So a large school rucksack would hold ten times this amount. *1 litre*	B25
28	A	Reverse the calculation: $(3 \times 8) \div 4 \div 2 = 24 \div 4 \div 2 = 6 \div 2 = 3$	B3
29	E	The x-axis coordinates for the three points are: H = $^-$3, J = 4, K = $^-$4. E is the only option with these x-axis coordinates.	B23
30	B	Ian gets less than Kirsty so he gets 9 parts of the total. Ian gets £36 so each part is £36 ÷ 9 = £4. Kirsty gets 12 parts of the total or 12 × £4 = £48. (Or multiply the ratio by 4, which gives 12 : 9 = 48 : 36.)	B13
31	D	8 people swam 30−34 lengths and 2 people swam 35−39 lengths so 8 + 2 = 10 people swam 30 or more lengths.	B14
32	E	$43 + 11 + 14 - 7 + 6 - 9 + 2 = 60$	B2
33	B	$\frac{6}{12} = \frac{1}{2} = 50\%$	B12
34	C	<table><tr><th>Ten thousands</th><th>Thousands</th><th>Hundreds</th><th>Tens</th><th>Units</th></tr><tr><td>4</td><td>3</td><td>6</td><td>0</td><td>8</td></tr></table>	B1
35	C	'y is equal to $\frac{3}{4}$ of x' means '$y = \frac{3}{4}x$'. Rearrange all of the equations to look like '$y = \ldots$' Divide both sides of A by 4, multiply both sides of B by x, divide both sides of C by 3, D stays the same and multiply both sides of E by $\frac{3}{4}$. C says '$y = \frac{4}{3}x$'.	B8
36	A	$\frac{4}{5} \times 400 = 400 \div 5 \times 4 = 80 \times 4 = 320$	B10
37	D	There are 9 small triangles, each with an area of $500\,mm^2$. $9 \times 500\,mm^2 = 4500\,mm^2 = 45\,cm^2$ $(1\,cm^2 = 10\,mm \times 10\,mm = 100\,mm^2)$	B3
38	B	1 m 10 cm = 110 cm = (110 ÷ 2.5 inches) = 44 inches = 3 feet 8 inches, so answer B is the closest	B25
39	D	1.5 litre = 1500 millilitres $\frac{1250}{1500} = \frac{250}{300} = \frac{5}{6}$	B10
40	B	$192 \times \frac{5}{8} = 192 \div 8 \times 5 = 24 \times 5 = 120$ international flights so $192 - 120 = 72$ domestic flights (Or if $\frac{5}{8}$ international flights, $\frac{3}{8}$ are domestic flights so $192 \times \frac{3}{8} = 192 \div 8 \times 3 = 24 \times 3 = 72$ domestic flights.)	B10
41	C	45 CDs are sold on Day 2. 15 CDs are sold on Day 4. $45 - 15 = 30$	B14
42	D	Temperature °C $^-11$ $^-10$ $^-9$ $^-8$ $^-7$ $^-6$ $^-5$ $^-4$ $^-3$ $^-2$ $^-1$ 0 1 Moscow has the lowest temperature because $^-11$ is the lowest of the numbers.	B6
43	E	E is the only choice where both sentences are correct.<table><tr><th>Marble</th><th>Probability</th><th>Odds</th></tr><tr><td>Red</td><td>$\frac{1}{6}$</td><td>less than even</td></tr><tr><td>Green</td><td>$\frac{2}{6} = \frac{1}{3}$</td><td>less than even</td></tr><tr><td>Yellow</td><td>$\frac{3}{6} = \frac{1}{2}$</td><td>even</td></tr></table>	B16
44	A	Total number of pencils: $2 + 3 + 4 + 5 + 6 = 20$ Number of pencils that are not red: $20 - 3 = 17$	B16
45	A	12 hour: 1 2 3 4 5 6 7 8 9 10 11 12 1 2 3 4 5 6 7 8 9 10 11 12 24 hour: 1 2 3 4 5 6 7 8 9 10 11 12 13 14 15 16 17 18 19 20 21 22 23 24 (Or add 12 hours to 9:45, i.e. 12:00 + 9:45 = 21:45.)	B27
46	B	100 − 16 = 84p, 84 ÷ 6 = 14p	B4
47	D	810 000 ÷ 27	B15
48	C	Angle y is less than 90° (a right angle) and greater than 45°. C is the only option that is greater than 45° and less than 90°.	B19

Question number	Answer		
49	E	These dimensions (in cm) would give an area of 36 cm²: 1×36, 2×18, 3×12, 4×9, 6×6 The perimeters of these rectangles are: 74 cm, 40 cm, 30 cm, 26 cm, 24 cm	B20
50	D	The sequence can be calculated by $1 = 1$ $1 + (1 \times 6) = 1 + 6 = 7$ $1 + (1 \times 6) + (2 \times 6) = 1 + 6 + 12 = 19$ $1 + (1 \times 6) + (2 \times 6) + (3 \times 6) = 1 + 6 + 12 + 18 = 37$ There are 37 hexagons in the 4th shape. 1 $1 + (1 \times 6)$ $1 + (1 \times 6) + (2 \times 6)$ $1 + (1 \times 6) + (2 \times 6) + (3 \times$	B7

Test 2

1	B	$144 \div 7 = 20$ remainder 4	B3
2	E	$\begin{array}{r} 60\,000 \\ 7\,000 \\ 800 \\ +\quad 90 \\ \hline 67\,890 \end{array}$	B1
3	A	Unknown angle in triangle $= 180° - r - s = 180° - 49° - 37° = 94°$ $q = 360° - 94° = 266°$	B18
4	C	How many parts of 5 m are there in the driveway? $12.5\,\text{m} \div 5\,\text{m} = 2.5$ How long will the scale drawing be if each part is 2 cm long? $2\,\text{cm} \times 2.5 = 5\,\text{cm}$ (Or 2 cm : 5 m so 1 cm : 2.5 m so 5 cm : 12.5 m.)	B3
5	D	Convert all the options to fractions of 100. All except option D are equal to $\frac{3}{4}$ of 100. $0.075 = \frac{75}{1000} = \frac{3}{40}$ D is $\frac{3}{40}$ of 100.	B10
6	B	The percentage who have not replied is $100\% - 85\% = 15\%$. 15% of 780 (the number of pupils) $= 0.15 \times 780 = 117$	B12
7	B	$(56 \times 10\text{p}) + (75 \times 5\text{p}) = 560\text{p} + 375\text{p} = 935\text{p} = £9.35$	B4
8	A	Friday = 8 hrs, Thursday = $8 - 2 = 6$ hrs, Wednesday = $6 \div 3 = 2$ hrs, Tuesday = $2 \times 2 = 4$ hrs	B4
9	C	$2005 = 23$ $2006 = 23 \times 2 = 46$ $2007 = 46 \times 2 = 92$	B3
10	E	$\frac{1}{2} \times 6\,\text{cm} \times 6\,\text{cm} = 3 \times 6\,\text{cm}^2 = 18\,\text{cm}^2$	B20
11	A	There is a common difference of 6 between numbers along each row and along each column so $110 + 6 = 116$.	B7
12	D	To find what percentage of cars have three doors, subtract the known percentages in the pie chart from 100: $100\% - 35\% - 30\% - 20\% = 15\%$ What is 15% of 60 cars? $\frac{15}{100} \times 60 = 9$ (Or 10% of 60 + 5% of 60 = 6 + 3.)	B12
13	C	$532 \div 28 = 19$	B3
14	E	$2\,\text{m}\,8\,\text{cm} = 208\,\text{cm}$, $208 \div 2 = 104\,\text{cm}$	B3
15	B	$24 \times 25\,\text{cm} \times 25\,\text{cm} = 15\,000\,\text{cm}^2 = 1.5\,\text{m}^2$ because $1\,\text{m}^2 = 100\,\text{cm}^2 \times 100\,\text{cm}^2$ (Or there are sixteen 25 cm × 25 cm tiles in 1 m², so divide the number of white tiles by sixteen.)	B20
16	D	There are 18 even numbers between 1 and 36 but considering the number zero, then 18 numbers out of 37 are even.	B16
17	B	12 is a multiple of 6 so the answer must be a multiple of 12. 24 is the only answer that is a multiple of 12.	B5
18	C	A net of a closed cube can be cut out and folded to form a 3-D box without any of the sides overlapping and without there being any sides missing. The cube made from E has two sides missing while A, B and D have overlapping sides.	B21

Question number	Answer		
19	D	Reverse the calculation: $(99 + 7) \div 2$	B9
20	C	Morag earns $5 \times £x$ during the week and $2 \times £x$ each day of the weekend. $(5 \times £x) + (2 \times £x) + (2 \times £x) = £5x + £2x + £2x = £9x$	B8
21	C	The next part of the sequence goes $16 - 9 = 7$, then $25 - 16 = 9$. 9 is not a prime number.	B7
22	E	The Petrol Station is 4.5 units to the right and 2 units up.	B23
23	A	Each child costs $£780 - £150 = £630$. 3 adults at $£780 = £2340$; 2 children at $£630 = £1260$. $£2340 + £1260 = £3600$	B4
24	D	4, 8, 12, 16, 20, 24, … are the multiples of 4. 5, 10, 15, 20, 25, … are the multiples of 5.	B5
25	E	There are 6 children with $10-14$ marks and 4 children with $15-19$ marks, so there are $6 + 4 = 10$ children with fewer than 20 marks.	B14
26	B	4.05 and 4.1 are the lowest values. Convert both to fractions and compare. $4.05 = 4\frac{5}{100}$ $4.1 = 4\frac{1}{10} = 4\frac{10}{100}$ ($0.05 = \frac{5}{100}$ is lower than $0.1 = \frac{10}{100}$)	B10
27	B	Sum all the costs for the class. $£30 + £2.50 + £1.10 + £3.50 + £4.75 + £2.15 + £1.65$	B2
28	E	Starting from the top left, add up all the sides. Calculate the missing sides first then sum all the sides of the shape. $(5 + 1.5 + 2 + 1.5 + 2 + 7 + 1 + 1 + 3 + 1 + 5 + 7)$ m	B20
29	D	Half of $£12.60 = £6.30$, half of $£6.30 = £3.15$. The price you pay is $£12.60 - £3.15 = £9.45$. The change you receive is $£10.00 - £9.45 = £0.55$.	B4
30	A	10% of $£540 = £54$ 30% of $£540 = 3 \times 10\%$ of $£540 = 3 \times £54 = £162$ $£540 - £162 = £378$	B12
31	C	(see table below)	B16

Question 31 table

Dice roll	Probability	Odds
Odd number	$\frac{3}{6} = \frac{1}{2}$	even
Number less than 6	$\frac{5}{6}$	more than even
Prime number	$\frac{3}{6} = \frac{1}{2}$	even
Number less than seven	$\frac{6}{6} = 1$	certain

Question number	Answer		
32	D	For a parallelogram, QT must be parallel to RS and equal in length to RS (similarly, ST must be parallel to RQ and the same length as RQ).	B19
33	E	The missing number is halfway between 11.02 and 15.43. $(15.43 + 11.02) \div 2 = 13.225 = 13.23$ to 2 decimal places (Or the amounts in the 'pounds to kg' column are going up by approximately the same amount each time so the amounts in the 'kg to pounds' column will also go up by approximately the same amount each time. The difference between rows 7 and 8 in the 'kg to pounds' column is: $17.64 - 15.43 = 2.21$ lb. So row 6 in the 'kg to pounds' column is: $11.02 + 2.21 = 13.23$ lb.)	B7

Question number	Answer		
34	E	$110 - 89 = 21$ (the total number of pupils minus the total of all the other instruments added together)	B14
35	C	The octagon, as it has the highest number of sides. As the number of sides increases, the internal angles get bigger.	B19
36	A	$9x + 9 = 54$ (add $4x$ to both sides) $9x = 45$ (subtract 9 from both sides) $x = 5$ (divide both sides by 9)	B8
37	B	$520 - 433 = 87$	B2
38	C	The coffee weighs 0.5 kg, a bag of sugar weighs 0.5 to 2 kg and a chicken may weigh around 2 to 3 kg. An estimate of the minimum total weight of the shopping is $0.5 + 0.5 + 2 = 3$ kg. The maximum total weight could be $0.5 + 2 + 3 = 5.5$ kg. So the weight is probably between 3 kg and 5.5 kg.	B25
39	E	The path turns left, left then right so the answer must be A or E. The last part of the path is only 2 squares forward so choose option E.	B17
40	D	The median is the middle number when the amounts are placed in order.	B15
41	C	The mean is 6, which was measured over 7 days so the total number of cups is $7 \times 6 = 42$. Number of cups on Tuesday $= 42 - 32$ (the total number of cups for all other days) $= 10$.	B15
42	C	The second sort is to ask 'Can the material be recycled?' which must apply to all of the materials.	B14
43	B	Note that €32 − €28 = €4, so the equivalent of €4 is £20 − £17.50 = £2.50.	B2
44	E	Use trial and error: $1 \times 1 \times 1 = 1$, $2 \times 2 \times 2 = 8$, etc. (Or use the reverse process which is to find the cube root of the number: $\sqrt[3]{125} = 5$)	B6
45	A	Capacity $= 10 \text{ cm} \times 6 \text{ cm} \times 4 \text{ cm} = 240 \text{ cm}^3$	B22
46	D	The total number of houses on the street is $34 + 16 = 50$. $\frac{34}{50} = \frac{17}{25}$	B10
47	E	The shape has one line of symmetry (so eliminate A, B and C) and no sides are parallel (so eliminate D).	B19
48	D	The smallest division of the scale is 0.2 kg. The person weighs 30.4 kg with the coat on (from the picture). $30.4 - 0.8 = 29.6$ kg	B2
49	E	$(5 \times 7) - (7 \times 4) + (3 \times 9) = 35 - 28 + 27 = 34$	B8
50	C	All the other words have a vertical line of symmetry, which splits the word into mirrored halves, through the middle letter. WOW TOT SOS MUM AXA	B24

Test 3

Question number	Answer		
1	C	Reverse the calculation: $(33 - 4) \times 2 = 29 \times 2 = 58$	B5
2	B	$\frac{24}{90} = \frac{4}{15}$	B10
3	C	$6 \text{ cm} \times 4 \text{ cm} = 24 \text{ cm}^2$	B20
4	E	$24 : 32 = 3 : 4$ (Divide by the highest common factor, 8)	B13
5	B	The second sort of the chocolates is to ask 'Does it contain a nut?' and this must be applied to all of the chocolates.	B14
6	D	Children having 1 sibling is represented by a quarter of the pie chart. $\frac{1}{4} \times 32 = 8$	B10
7	A	Calculate a then b then the square with the question mark: $47 - 19 - 13 = 15$, $47 - 15 - 14 = 18$, $47 - 18 - 18 = 11$ (Or calculate c then d then the square with the question mark.)	B2

Question number	Answer		
8	E	$198 - 173 = 25$ (the difference between the highest value and lowest value)	B15
9	D	All the shapes have a perimeter of 8 m except D which has a perimeter of 13 m.	B20
10	C	25, 49 and 64 are square numbers. 27 and 64 are cube numbers.	B6
11	C	This shape has 8 unequal sides, so it is an octagon and is irregular.	B19
12	C	The total number of children is $13 + 16 = 29$. The fraction of boys in the nursery is $\frac{13}{29}$.	B10
13	E	The only number between 20 and 22 is 21, which is not a prime number so there is no chance of this statement happening. All the other statements have some chance of happening.	B16
14	C	The plane cannot go forward 5 then turn left without hitting a hangar (eliminate B). Going forward then turning right takes the plane off the map (eliminate A and D). Option E leaves the plane in the middle of the map. Option C brings the plane to the terminal.	B17
15	D	3 hours $= 3 \times 60$ minutes $= 180$ minutes $\frac{15}{180} = \frac{1}{12}$	B10
16	B	$3 \times 14 \times £3.20 = £134.40$ (number of lessons per week $\times$ number of weeks $\times$ cost per lesson)	B3
17	A	$13 \div 2 = 6.5\,cm^2$	B20
18	E	1 cm : 6 m = 3 cm : 18 m (multiply both sides of the ratio by 3)	B13
19	COX	Only this word can have a line drawn through the middle of each letter which splits the word into mirrored halves.	B24
20	E	$\frac{1}{4} \times 36 = \frac{36}{4} = 9$ (one-quarter of 36 is 9) If three-quarters of the class said "Yes" then one-quarter must have said "No".	B10
21	D	$(£2.00) + (3 \times 50p) + (7 \times 5p) + (6 \times 1p) = £2 + £1.50 + 35p + 6p = £3.91$	B2
22	B	$\frac{3}{7} \times 63 = 63 \div 7 \times 3 = 9 \times 3 = 27$	B10
23	E	21 is already divisible by 7 so the answer is any multiple of 21. Only 21 is a multiple of 21 in this list.	B5
24	A	The sides of this box are 2 cm, 3 cm and 5 cm. The volume of the box is $2\,cm \times 3\,cm \times 5\,cm = 30\,cm^3$.	B22
25	C	If Edward is x years old in 5 years' time then today he is $(x - 5)$ years old. 4 years ago he was $(x - 5 - 4)$ years old $= (x - 9)$ years old.	B8
26	D	$\frac{3}{10}$ of 360 = 0.3 of 360 = 30% of 360 = 108 $(3 \times \frac{1}{10} \times 360 = 3 \times 36 = 108)$ $\frac{1}{3} \times 360 = \frac{360}{3} = 120$ (this is the largest value)	B10
27	B	The angle shown is less than a right angle i.e. less than 90°. The angle appears close to half the size of a right angle, which is 45°. Of the three angles less than 90°, only 40° is close to 45°.	B18
28	A	$700 \times 56 = 39\,200$	B3
29	C	The modal colour is red because more pupils chose red than any other colour (tallest bar).	B15
30	E	$£18.23 - £1.55 = £16.68$ (original price minus discount)	B2
31	C	A stride is usually not quite a metre in length. A car is approximately 3 metres. Use these facts to estimate a length for the drive (between 12 and 20 m) compare the values with the ones given. 4 m, 2000 mm (2 m) and 240 cm (2.4 m) are too small. 200 m is too large.	B25
32	D	The number of matches for each shape follows this sequence: 4, 4 + 8, 4 + 8 + 12, 4 + 8 + 12 + 16, … or (1×4), $(1 \times 4) + (2 \times 4)$, $(1 \times 4) + (2 \times 4) + (3 \times 4)$, $(1 \times 4) + (2 \times 4) + (3 \times 4) + (4 \times 4)$, … or 4, 12, 24, 40, …	B7
33	A	$21 \times 5 \div 3 = 35$	B9
34	D	(see table below)	B1

Ten thousands	Thousands	Hundreds	Tens	Units
3	1	5	0	9

Question number	Answer		
35	E	If you add f to both sides of equation E you get: $f + 2g = 4h + 2f$ All the other equations can be made to look like $f + 2g = 4h$ by adding or subtracting appropriate values to or from both sides.	B8
36	B	$\frac{4}{9} \times 72 = 72 \div 9 \times 4 = 8 \times 4 = 32$ (the number of shops selling food or drinks) $72 - 32 = 40$ (the number of shops not selling food or drinks)	B10
37	B	<table><tr><td>Shape</td><td>Pairs of parallel sides</td></tr><tr><td>Kite</td><td>0</td></tr><tr><td>Trapezium</td><td>1</td></tr><tr><td>Regular pentagon</td><td>0</td></tr><tr><td>Regular hexagon</td><td>3</td></tr><tr><td>Regular octagon</td><td>4</td></tr></table>	B19
38	A	The team won $8 + 12 + 5 = 25$. The team drew $9 + 6 + 5 = 20$. The total number of games not lost (either won or drawn) $= 25 + 20 = 45$.	B14
39	D	After one year, Karen is $(150 + k)$ cm tall and Pippa is $(150 + p)$ cm tall. The difference in their heights is $(150 + p) - (150 + k) = 150 - 150 + p - k = p - k$ (because Pippa is taller). The difference between Karen's height and Pippa's height increases by $(p - k)$ cm each year so after 4 years the difference is 4 times this amount $= 4 \times (p - k) = 4(p - k)$.	B8
40	B	The angle that separates line G from line M is $90°$. These lines are perpendicular to each other. All the other statements are false.	B17
41	E	Each grid square is 0.1 units across. The cross lies 6 squares to the right and 3 squares up from the starting point. The starting point of the graph is (6, 6). The coordinates are therefore: $6 + (6 \times 0.1) = 6.6$ (in the x direction) and $6 + (3 \times 0.1) = 6.3$ (in the y direction) or (6.6, 6.3)	B23
42	E	The amounts in the 'feet to m' column are going up by approximately the same amount each time so the amounts in the 'm to feet' column will also go up by approximately the same amount each time. The difference between elements 6 and 7 in the 'm to feet' column is: $22.97 - 19.68 = 3.29$ ft. So the element 5 in the 'm to feet' column is: $19.68 - 3.29 = 16.39$ ft (which is closest to 16.40 ft).	B25
43	A	The digit in the third decimal place is 6 so the number rounds up to 7.00 to 2 decimal places. (Note that the correct answer must include the two zeros, to show the number is accurate to 2 decimal places.)	B1
44	S	Shape S has one interior angle that is greater than $180°$.	B19
45	E	The y-axis coordinates for the three points are: X = 6, Y = 2, Z = 1. E is the only option with these y-axis coordinates.	B23
46	A	The total number of children $= 62 + 65 = 127$ Subtract the number of children doing other jobs to find the remainder, who are doing the front of house: $127 - 73 - 48 = 6$	B4
47	D	There are 3 full crisp packets and 1 half crisp packet in the pictogram for Prawn Cocktail. This stands for $(3 \times 8) + (1 \times 4) = 24 + 4 = 28$ children.	B14
48	A	$\frac{1}{7} + \frac{2}{7} = \frac{3}{7}$ of the pupils take a bus or car so $\frac{4}{7}$ must walk. $\frac{4}{7} \times 35 = 4 \times \frac{1}{7} \times 35 = 4 \times 5 = 20$	B10
49	E	This is just one example of a possible route, further paths are available..	
50	B	Lauren's bags $= (1 \times 440\,g) + (2 \times 150\,g) = 440\,g + 300\,g = 740\,g$ Peter's bags $= \frac{1}{2} \times$ Lauren's bags $= \frac{1}{2} \times 740\,g = \frac{740}{2}g = 370\,g$	B4

Question number	Answer		
1	D	$\frac{23}{60}$ cannot be simplified any further. Convert all of the fractions in the list to 60ths and see which numerator has the closest value to 23. The fractions are: $\frac{30}{60}, \frac{20}{60}, \frac{15}{60}, \frac{24}{60}$ and $\frac{25}{60}$. $\frac{2}{5} = \frac{24}{60}$ is the closest fraction in the list to $\frac{23}{60}$. (Or note that the closest fractions to $\frac{23}{60}$ are $\frac{24}{60}$ and $\frac{22}{60}$. $\frac{22}{60} = \frac{11}{30}$. $\frac{24}{60} = \frac{4}{10} = \frac{2}{5}$.)	B10
2	D	The area of the hexagon is 6 times the area of each small triangle. The area of each small triangle is: $\frac{1}{2} \times$ base $\times$ height $= \frac{1}{2} \times x \times y$ So the total area $= 6 \times$ area of small triangle $= 6 \times \frac{1}{2} \times x \times y$ $= \frac{6}{2} xy$ $= 3xy$	B20
3	B	There are 2 bus trips every day and 5 days of going to school. The total bus fares $= 2 \times 5 \times £0.57$ $= 10 \times £0.57$	B3
4	A	The percentage of pupils driven to school is 100% minus the total of the rest of the pie chart. $100\% - 20\% - 30\% - 8\% = 100\% - 58\% = 42\%$ 42% of pupils are driven. $\frac{42}{100} \times 350 = \frac{42}{10} \times 35 = \frac{42}{2} \times 7 = 21 \times 7 = 147$	B14
5	C	$14 \times 26 = 10 \times 26 + 4 \times 26 = 260 + 104 = 364$	B4
6	E	$(92 \div 4) \times 5 = 23 \times 5 = 115$	B9
7	A	There are 28 shaded triangles and 12 white triangles (40 triangles in total) all of which are the same size. $\frac{28}{40} = \frac{7}{10} = \frac{70}{100} = 70\%$	B12
8	C	Yearly cost of gym $= 12 \times$ monthly membership $= 12x$ Yearly cost of Pilates $= 52 \times$ weekly class cost $= 52y$ Total cost $= 12x + 52y$	B8
9	B	$43 \times £25 = £1075$	B3
10	B	The fraction of reference books in the library is 1 minus the total of the other books: $1 - \frac{1}{5} - \frac{2}{5} = \frac{2}{5}$ $\frac{1}{5} \times 240 = \frac{240}{5} = 48$ $\frac{2}{5} \times 240 = 2 \times \frac{1}{5} \times 240 = 96$	B10
11	D	Calculate a then the square with the question mark. $33 - 9 - 13 = 11, 33 - 11 - 10 = 12$	B2
12	C	The computer checks e-mails every 5 minutes and checks news updates every 7 minutes. The error message occurs at a time which is a multiple of both 5 and 7. The lowest common multiple of 5 and 7 is 35, so every 35 minutes there is an error message. In one hour there is one error message. The second error message occurs at 2×35 minutes $= 70$ minutes $= 1$ hour 10 minutes, the third error message occurs at 3×35 minutes $= 105$ minutes $= 1$ hour 45 minutes, etc. In 5 hours there are $5 \times 60 = 300$ minutes. $\frac{300}{35} = \frac{60}{7} = 8.57...$ The error message occurs 8 times.	B4
13	C	$5 \times £1.20 + 4 \times £0.95 + 3 \times £0.75 + 6 \times £0.50 + 2 \times £1.40$ $= £6.00 + £3.80 + £2.25 + £3.00 + £2.80$ $= £17.85$	B4
14	A	The team drew $3 + 2 + 8 = 13$ games. The team lost $1 + 5 + 0 = 6$ games. The total number of games either drawn or lost $= 13 + 6 = 19$.	B14
15	E	$6.5 \times 500 = 3250$	B3
16	E	The number of pupils liking apples best is represented in the pictogram by one whole banana plus one part banana. One whole banana $= 6$ children One part banana $=$ less than 6 children (i.e. 1 to 5 children) So the number of children liking apples best must be between $6 + 1$ and $6 + 5$, or between 7 and 11 children. The only option between 7 and 11 is answer E.	B14

17	C	This shape has 8 unequal sides therefore it must be an irregular octagon.	B19
18	C	1 cm represents 25 000 cm (the scale is 1 : 25 000). 25 000 cm = $\frac{25\,000}{100}$ m = 250 m = $\frac{250}{1000}$ km = 0.25 km	B13
19	B	200 000 3 000 80 + 1 ‾‾‾‾‾‾ 203 081	B1
20	D	0.5 litres is half the size of most orange juice containers, or slightly less than 1 pint. A milk bottle may contain 0.5 litres (an egg cup will contain about 50 millilitres and a kettle will contain about 5 litres).	B25
21	B	Total cost − deposit = £225 − £50 = £175 to be paid by the monthly savings. It will take £175 ÷ £35 = 5 months.	B4
22	A	22 cm − (2 × 10 cm) = 22 cm − 20 cm = 2 cm 2 × unknown side = 2 cm unknown side = 1 cm Area of rectangle = length × width = 10 cm × 1 cm = 10 cm²	B20
23	A	Each grid square is 0.1 units across. The cross lies 2 squares to the right and 4 squares up from the starting point. The starting point of the graph is (2, 2). The coordinates are therefore: 2 + (2 × 0.1) = 2.2 (in the x direction) and 2 + (4 × 0.1) = 2.4 (in the y direction) or (2.2, 2.4)	B23
24	E	The plane first turns left (eliminates A and C). It must then turn right (eliminate D) then right again (eliminate B).	B17
25	B	1 foot = 12 inches ≈ 30 cm 6 feet ≈ 6 × 30 cm = 180 cm = 1.8 m 3 inches ≈ $\frac{3}{12}$ × 30 cm = $\frac{1}{4}$ × 30 cm = 7.5 cm So 6 feet 3 inches ≈ 1.8 m + 0.075 m = 1.875 m. This is closest to 1.9 m.	B25
26	C	2.2 kg = 2200 g 400 g out of 2200 g = $\frac{4}{22}$ = $\frac{2}{11}$	B10
27	B	Note that the perimeter of this shape is just $2 \times (a + c) + 2 \times (b + d)$ because if you moved the sides you could make a rectangle of width $a + c$ and length $b + d$. The perimeter of both shapes is therefore the same.	B20
28	NOS	Turn the paper upside down and see which one forms a word.	B23
29	A	If Nankunda was x years old six years ago, today she is $x + 6$ years old. In seven years time she will be $x + 6 + 7 = x + 13$ years old.	B8
30	E	The first eight square numbers are 1, 4, 9, 16, 25, 36, 49 and 64. The first four cube numbers are 1, 8, 27 and 64. So 64 is both a cube number and a square number. (Or 64 = 4 × 4 × 4 = 8 × 8.)	B6
31	D	Line S is perpendicular to line V.	B17
32	A	There were 50 magazines sold on Wednesday and 25 magazines sold on Monday. There were 50 − 25 = 25 more magazines sold on Wednesday than on Monday.	B14
33	C	Convert all numbers to decimals and then compare. 0.95 94.3% = $\frac{94.3}{100}$ = 0.943 $\frac{24}{25}$ = $\frac{96}{100}$ = 0.96 94.29% = $\frac{94.29}{100}$ = 0.9429 $\frac{24}{27}$ = $\frac{8}{9}$ = 0.888…	B11

Question number	Answer		
34	A	The temperature that appears the most often is 28°C (4 times).	B15
35	B	The x-axis coordinates for the three points are: M = 4, N = 6, P = 3. B is the only option with these x-axis coordinates.	B23
36	E	36 : 20 = 9 : 5 = 18 : 10 = 27 : 15 = 45 : 25 = 54 : 30	B13
37	C	David's age today is his age in two years' time minus two years = 14 − 2 = 12 years. David's sister's age is one third David's age = 12 ÷ 3 = 4 years.	B4
38	D	The path may also go in the opposite direction, so may start from either point (end to start or start to end).	
39	C	Angle r is 60° (because it is the internal angle of an equilateral triangle). Angle q is 120° (because angles on a straight line add to 180°). p is the same as angle q (opposite angles in a parallelogram are equal).	B19
40	A	The larger shape can be split into four complete hexagons. Each hexagon can be split into six of the small triangles. $4 \times 6 = 24$	B19
41	B	$\frac{40}{100} \times £38.50 = \frac{2}{5} \times £38.50 = £38.50 \div 5 \times 2 = £7.70 \times 2 = £15.40$ £38.50 − £15.40 = £23.10	B12
42	D	432 − 26 − 217 = 189	B2
43	C	20 − 8 = 12 pieces left $\frac{12}{20} = 0.60 = 60\%$	B12
44	A	9 − 0 = 9 (the highest value minus the lowest value)	B15
45	B	(see table below)	B21
46	D		B23
47	E	The difference between ⁺8°C and ⁻3°C is 11°C.	B6
48	D	Look at the cost of all the items in the list and compare them. Let the cost of a ruler or an eraser be r and the cost of a pencil be p. A costs $5r$. B costs $2r + 6p$. C costs $4r + 2p$. D costs $4r + 4p$. E costs $4r + 2p$. C and E are the same so neither can be the odd one out. A and B are the same if $r = p$. D is $2p$ more than C and E, so it must be the odd one out.	B8
49	E	7.0 has precisely the same value as 7 and so has the closest value to 7.	B1
50	B	8 goals were scored in 46−60 minutes, 3 goals were scored in 61−75 minutes and 5 goals were scored in 76−90 minutes. The total number of goals scored after 45 minutes is 8 + 3 + 5 = 16 goals	B14

Question 45 table:

Shape	Number of edges	Number of faces
A	12	6
B	8	5
C	18	8
D	9	5
E	12	8

Bond NEW EDITION

11⁺ Test Papers

Maths

Answer sheets for Multiple-choice Tests

The answer sheets for Bond 11⁺ Test papers Multiple-choice version are in this booklet. Please ensure you are using the correct answer sheet for the test you are taking.

Text © Andrew Baines 2007
Original illustrations © Nelson Thornes Ltd 2007

First published in 2003 by:
Nelson Thornes Ltd

This edition published in 2007 by:
Nelson Thornes Ltd, Delta Place, 27 Bath Road
CHELTENHAM GL53 7TH, United Kingdom

07 08 09 10 11 / 10 9 8 7 6 5 4 3 2 1

A catalogue record for this book is available from the British Library

ISBN 978 0 7487 8482 0

Page make-up by Tech Set Ltd

Printed and bound in Croatia by Zrinski

Published by Nelson Thornes. Nelson Thornes is a Wolters Kluwer company, and is not associated in any way with NFER-Nelson.

Nelson Thornes
a Wolters Kluwer business

Bond 11⁺ Maths Test 1

Name

1
D
E
F
G
H

2
A
B
C
D
E

3
A
B
C
D
E

4
A
B
C
D
E

5
A
B
C
D
E

6
P
Q
R
S
T

7
A
B
C
D
E

8
A
B
C
D
E

9
A
B
C
D
E

10
A
B
C
D
E

11
A
B
C
D
E

12
A
B
C
D
E

13
A
B
C
D
E

14
A
B
C
D
E

15
A
B
C
D
E

16
A
B
C
D
E

17
A
B
C
D
E

18
A
B
C
D
E

19
A
B
C
D
E

20
A
B
C
D
E

21
A
B
C
D
E

22
A
B
C
D
E

23
A
B
C
D
E

24
A
B
C
D
E

25
A
B
C
D
E

26
A
B
C
D
E

27
A
B
C
D
E

28
A
B
C
D
E

29
A
B
C
D
E

30
A
B
C
D
E

31
A
B
C
D
E

32
A
B
C
D
E

33
A
B
C
D
E

34
A
B
C
D
E

35
A
B
C
D
E

36
A
B
C
D
E

37
A
B
C
D
E

38
A
B
C
D
E

39
A
B
C
D
E

40
A
B
C
D
E

41
A
B
C
D
E

42
A
B
C
D
E

43
A
B
C
D
E

44
A
B
C
D
E

45
A
B
C
D
E

46
A
B
C
D
E

47
A
B
C
D
E

48
A
B
C
D
E

49
A
B
C
D
E

50
A
B
C
D
E

Bond 11⁺ Maths Test 2

Name

Nelson Thornes
a Wolters Kluwer business

Bond 11+ Maths Test 3

Name

| 1 | A B C D E | 2 | A B C D E | 3 | A B C D E | 4 | A B C D E | 5 | A B C D E | 6 | A B C D E | 7 | A B C D E |

| 8 | A B C D E | 9 | A B C D E | 10 | A B C D E | 11 | A B C D E | 12 | A B C D E | 13 | A B C D E | 14 | A B C D E |

| 15 | A B C D E | 16 | A B C D E | 17 | A B C D E | 18 | A B C D E | 19 | COX NON DAD MUM HIT | 20 | A B C D E | 21 | A B C D E |

| 22 | A B C D E | 23 | A B C D E | 24 | A B C D E | 25 | A B C D E | 26 | A B C D E | 27 | A B C D E | 28 | A B C D E |

| 29 | A B C D E | 30 | A B C D E | 31 | A B C D E | 32 | A B C D E | 33 | A B C D E | 34 | A B C D E | 35 | A B C D E |

| 36 | A B C D E | 37 | A B C D E | 38 | A B C D E | 39 | A B C D E | 40 | A B C D E | 41 | A B C D E | 42 | A B C D E |

| 43 | A B C D E | 44 | R S T U V | 45 | A B C D E | 46 | A B C D E | 47 | A B C D E | 48 | A B C D E | 49 | A B C D E | 50 | A B C D E |

Bond 11+ Maths Test 4

Name

1 A B C D E

2 A B C D E

3 A B C D E

4 A B C D E

5 A B C D E

6 A B C D E

7 A B C D E

8 A B C D E

9 A B C D E

10 A B C D E

11 A B C D E

12 A B C D E

13 A B C D E

14 A B C D E

15 A B C D E

16 A B C D E

17 A B C D E

18 A B C D E

19 A B C D E

20 A B C D E

21 A B C D E

22 A B C D E

23 A B C D E

24 A B C D E

25 A B C D E

26 A B C D E

27 A B C D E

28 NOZE NOS HOSE ICON TON

29 A B C D E

30 A B C D E

31 A B C D E

32 A B C D E

33 A B C D E

34 A B C D E

35 A B C D E

36 A B C D E

37 A B C D E

38 A B C D E

39 A B C D E

40 A B C D E

41 A B C D E

42 A B C D E

43 A B C D E

44 A B C D E

45 A B C D E

46 A B C D E

47 A B C D E

48 A B C D E

49 A B C D E

50 A B C D E

Notes

Notes

Notes

Bond NEW EDITION

11+ Test Papers

Maths

Multiple-choice Test 1

Read the following:

- Do not begin the test or open this booklet until told to do so.

- Work as quickly and as carefully as you can.

- Answers should be marked in pencil in the answer booklet provided, not in this test booklet.

- You may do rough working on a separate sheet of paper.

- If you make a mistake rub out the mistake and write the new answer clearly.

- Be careful to keep your place in the accompanying answer booklet.

- You will have 50 minutes to complete the test.

- Calculators should not be used.

Text © Andrew Baines 2007
Original illustrations © Nelson Thornes Ltd 2007

The right of Andrew Baines to be identified as author of this work has been asserted by him in accordance with the Copyright, Designs and Patents Act 1988.

All rights reserved. No part of this publication may be reproduced or transmitted in any form or by any means, electronic or mechanical, including photocopying, recording or any information storage and retrieval system, without permission in writing from the publisher or under licence from the Copyright Licensing Agency Ltd, of Saffron House, 6–10 Kirby Street, London, EC1N 8TS.

Any person who commits any unauthorised act in relation to this publication may be liable to criminal prosecution and civil claims for damages.

First published in 2003 by:
Nelson Thornes Ltd

This edition published in 2007 by:
Nelson Thornes Ltd, Delta Place, 27 Bath Road
CHELTENHAM GL53 7TH, United Kingdom

07 08 09 10 11 / 10 9 8 7 6 5 4 3 2 1

A catalogue record for this book is available from the British Library

ISBN 978 0 7487 8482 0

Page make-up by Tech Set Ltd

Printed and bound in Croatia by Zrinski

Published by Nelson Thornes. Nelson Thornes is a Wolters Kluwer company, and is not associated in any way with NFER-Nelson.

Nelson Thornes

a Wolters Kluwer business

1

 D   E   F   G   H

Which quadrilateral does not have an obtuse angle?

2   Mrs Woodside is organising a school trip. Each child needs to pay £x for the transport.
Each child also has to pay £y for the accommodation. If there are 45 children going on the trip how much will the total payment be?

 A $45 + x + y$ B $45x + y$ C $x + 45y$ D $45(x + y)$ E $45xy$

3   If: $6x - 7 = 3x + 5$, what is x?

 A 9   B 4   C $\frac{2}{3}$ D $\frac{3}{4}$ E $\frac{4}{3}$

4   This graph is used to convert
kilograms to pounds.
Using the graph, write approximately
how many pounds is 200 kilograms.

 A 44 pounds   B 94 pounds

 C 404 pounds   D 400 pounds

 E 440 pounds

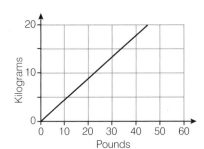

5

  A   B   C   D   E

Only one of the above diagrams is the net of a closed cuboid. Which net can be folded to form the closed cuboid?

6

 P   Q   R   S   T

Which of the above solids has an even number of vertices and an odd number of faces?

7   Jamie has a collection of antique comics. He has three worth £4.75 each, seven worth £3.20 each, and 12 worth £2 each. How much is his total collection worth?

 A £9.95   B £57.55   C £60.65   D £50.65   E £22

8   Look at this number line. What number does the arrow point to?

 7.4   7.5   7.6 ↓

 A 7.62   B 8   C 7.625   D 7.1   E 7.7

Continue to the next page

9 Pencils are sold in packs of five. The Art Department wants to buy 790 pencils. How many packs will need to be bought?

A   160   B   159   C   158   D   157   E   790

10 $5^4 = ?$

A $4 \times 4 \times 4 \times 4 \times 4$ B $5 \times 5 \times 5 \times 5$ C 5×4 D   54   E   45

11 Calculators are on special offer at £3.99. The Maths Department buys 125 calculators. What is the total cost?

A   £499.99   B   £997.50   C   £399   D   £498.75   E   £524.75

12 Azra collected the following data during a survey of her year group.

	Favourite racket sport		
	Badminton	Squash	Tennis
Boys	22	18	11
Girls	24	7	?

One hundred pupils completed the survey. How many girls gave tennis as their favourite sport?

A   18   B   11   C   19   D   100   E   0

13 3.344 670   What is this number to two decimal places?

A   3.35   B   3.3   C   3.34   D   3.344 670   E   3

14 A map of Belgium is drawn to a scale of 1:175 000. How many centimetres on the map would show 35 km?

A   35 cm   B   20 cm   C   17.5 cm   D   2 cm   E   3.5 cm

15 Which fraction has the smallest value?

A $\frac{4}{7}$ B $\frac{7}{12}$ C $\frac{4}{6}$ D $\frac{9}{16}$ E $\frac{5}{8}$

16 Which letter shows two prime numbers that add to make a cube number?

A   2 and 3   B   3 and 5   C   5 and 8   D   13 and 14   E   31 and 33

17 What are the coordinates of the Harbour Master?

A   (4, 6)   B   (4, 5.5)

C   (4.5, 6.5)   D   (3.5, 6.5)

E   (4, 6.5)

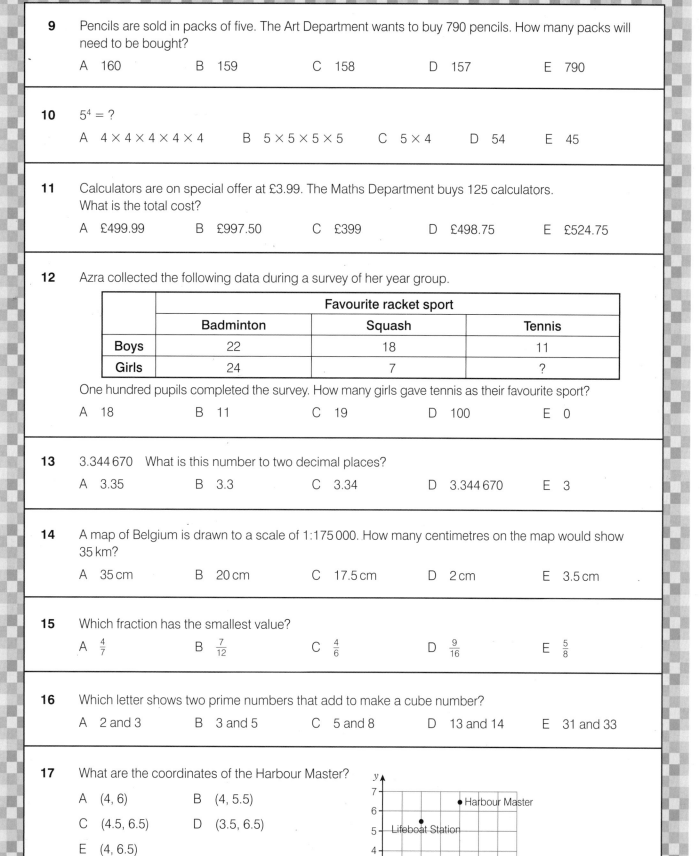

Please turn over

18

57	46	35
46	?	24
35	24	13

What is the missing number?

A　35　　　　　B　18　　　　C　24

D　0　　　　　E　57

19 Here is the plan of a room. How far is it all the way around the edge of the room?

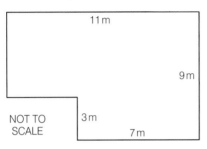

11 m

9 m

NOT TO SCALE

3 m

7 m

A　40 m

B　36 m

C　30 m

D　99 m

E　87 m

20 Year 6 at Abbey Primary School is going on an outing. The school minibus can take a maximum of 11 pupils. How many trips are needed to take all 57 pupils?

A　5　　　　　B　$\frac{2}{11}$　　　　C　11　　　　　D　6　　　　　E　57

21 These are the numbers of letters received by the school office each day for a week.

13　　　　　8　　　　　21　　　　　5　　　　　20

What is the median number of letters?

A　21　　　　　B　13　　　　　C　67　　　　　D　12　　　　　E　20

22 Which of these shapes has rotational symmetry?

  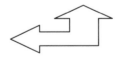

A　　　　　　　B　　　　　　　C　　　　　　　D　　　　　　　E

23 This is the plan of a room.
What is the area of the room?

A　56 m²　　　　　B　30 m²

C　51 m²　　　　　D　49 m²

E　50 m²

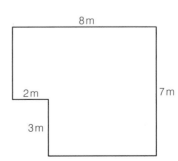

8 m

2 m

7 m

3 m

Continue to the next page

24

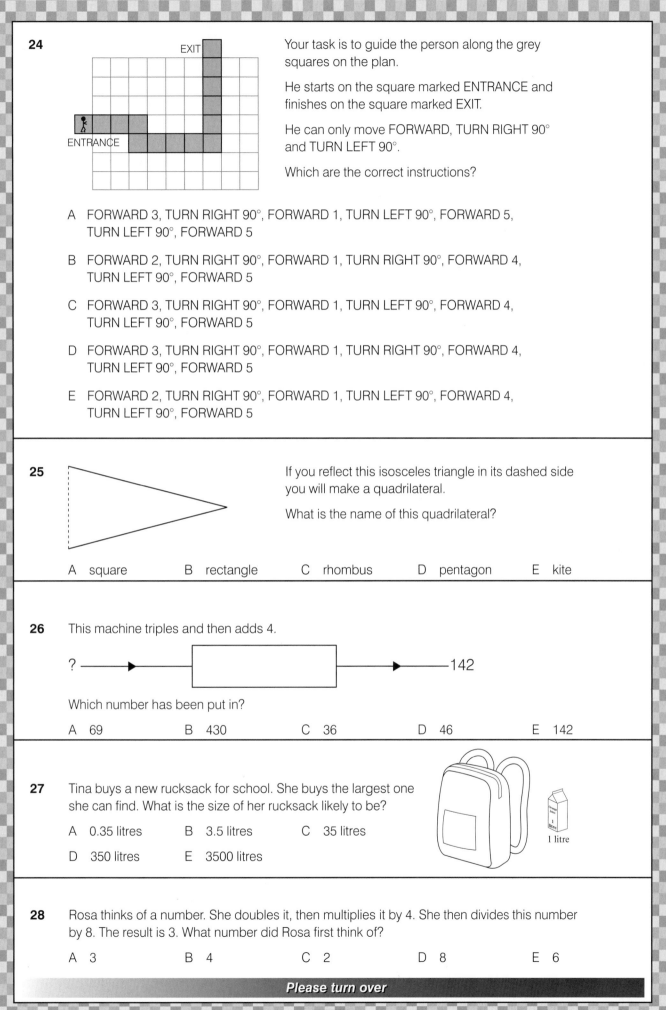

Your task is to guide the person along the grey squares on the plan.

He starts on the square marked ENTRANCE and finishes on the square marked EXIT.

He can only move FORWARD, TURN RIGHT 90° and TURN LEFT 90°.

Which are the correct instructions?

A   FORWARD 3, TURN RIGHT 90°, FORWARD 1, TURN LEFT 90°, FORWARD 5,
    TURN LEFT 90°, FORWARD 5

B   FORWARD 2, TURN RIGHT 90°, FORWARD 1, TURN RIGHT 90°, FORWARD 4,
    TURN LEFT 90°, FORWARD 5

C   FORWARD 3, TURN RIGHT 90°, FORWARD 1, TURN LEFT 90°, FORWARD 4,
    TURN LEFT 90°, FORWARD 5

D   FORWARD 3, TURN RIGHT 90°, FORWARD 1, TURN RIGHT 90°, FORWARD 4,
    TURN LEFT 90°, FORWARD 5

E   FORWARD 2, TURN RIGHT 90°, FORWARD 1, TURN LEFT 90°, FORWARD 4,
    TURN LEFT 90°, FORWARD 5

25

If you reflect this isosceles triangle in its dashed side you will make a quadrilateral.

What is the name of this quadrilateral?

A   square   B   rectangle   C   rhombus   D   pentagon   E   kite

---

26   This machine triples and then adds 4.

? ⟶ [   ] ⟶ 142

Which number has been put in?

A   69   B   430   C   36   D   46   E   142

---

27   Tina buys a new rucksack for school. She buys the largest one she can find. What is the size of her rucksack likely to be?

A   0.35 litres   B   3.5 litres   C   35 litres

D   350 litres   E   3500 litres

---

28   Rosa thinks of a number. She doubles it, then multiplies it by 4. She then divides this number by 8. The result is 3. What number did Rosa first think of?

A   3   B   4   C   2   D   8   E   6

29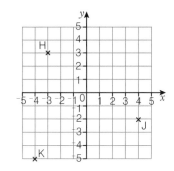

What are the coordinates of H, J and K?

A   H (3, ⁻3)   J (4, ⁻2)   K (4, 5)

B   H (⁻3, 3)   J (⁻2, 4)   K (⁻4, ⁻5)

C   H (3, ⁻3)   J (⁻2, 4)   K (⁻4, ⁻5)

D   H (⁻3, ⁻3)   J (4, 2)   K (⁻5, ⁻4)

E   H (⁻3, 3)   J (4, ⁻2)   K (⁻4, ⁻5)

---

30   Ian and Kirsty win a sum of money in a lottery. They share the money in the ratio of 12:9. Kirsty gets more than Ian. If Ian gets £36, how much does Kirsty get?

     A   £36   B   £48   C   £27   D   £12   E   £9

---

31   This bar chart shows the number of lengths swum in a sponsored swim.
How many people swam 30 or more lengths?

     A   8   B   2   C   16

     D   10   E   20

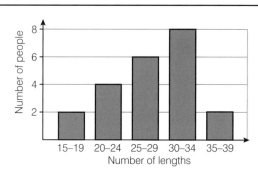

---

32   In 2002 there were 43 members of the school chess club. In 2003 there were 11 new members. In 2004 there were 14 new members and seven members who left. In 2005 there were six new members and nine members who left. In 2006 there were two new members.
How many members were there at the end of 2006?

     A   57   B   59   C   61   D   58   E   60

---

33   Here are the months of the year:

     January   February   March   April   May   June
     July   August   September   October   November   December

     As a percentage, how many months of the year have an even number of letters in their names?

     A   25%   B   50%   C   75%   D   100%   E   45%

---

34   43 608   What is this number in words?

     A   four thousand six hundred and eight

     B   four hundred and thirty-six thousand and eight

     C   forty-three thousand six hundred and eight

     D   four thousand three hundred and sixty-eight

     E   forty-three thousand and sixty-eight

---

35 y is equal to $\frac{3}{4}$ of x. Which of the following is incorrect?

     A $4y = 3x$ B $\frac{y}{x} = \frac{3}{4}$ C $3y = 4x$ D $y = \frac{3}{4}x$ E $x = \frac{4}{3}y$

---

36   400 vehicles pass Tara's house in one hour. $\frac{4}{5}$ of them are cars. How many of them are cars?

     A   320   B   300   C   500   D   350   E $\frac{1}{5}$

Continue to the next page

37 The area of the shaded triangle is 500 mm². What is the area of the largest triangle?

A 45 000 mm²　　B 4000 mm²　　C 4.5 cm²　　D 45 cm²　　E 450 cm²

---

38 Rashid is 1 metre 10 centimetres tall. Which is the closest to his height in feet and inches?

A 3 feet 4 inches　　　　B 3 feet 7 inches　　　　C 3 feet 10 inches

D 4 feet 1 inch　　　　E 4 feet 3 inches

---

39 1250 millilitres of a 1.500 litre bottle of cola is water. What fraction of the bottle is water?

A $\frac{2}{3}$　　　　B $\frac{3}{4}$　　　　C $\frac{4}{5}$　　　　D $\frac{5}{6}$　　　　E $\frac{6}{7}$

---

40 192 flights leave Newtown Airport each day. $\frac{5}{8}$ of them are international flights, the others are domestic flights. How many domestic flights leave Newtown Airport each day?

A 192　　　　B 72　　　　C 58　　　　D 120　　　　E 100

---

41 This bar chart shows the number of CDs sold by a shop in four days. How many more CDs were sold on Day 2 than on Day 4?

A 45　　　　B 15　　　　C 30

D 20　　　　E 40

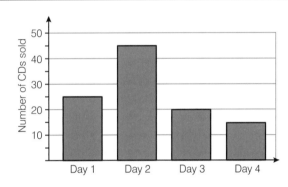

---

42 A newspaper showed the following temperatures on 1st February last year.

Amsterdam	2°C	Buenos Aires	21°C	Cairo	11°C	Cape Town	18°C
Delhi	19°C	Istanbul	4°C	Moscow	⁻11°C	Munich	⁻2°C
Nairobi	21°C	New York	⁻9°C	Tokyo	4°C	Vienna	3°C

Which place was the coldest on that day?

A Nairobi　　　　B Munich　　　　C New York　　　　D Moscow　　　　E Amsterdam

---

43 A bag contains one red marble, two green marbles and three yellow marbles.
You pick a marble at random from the bag. In which of these are both statements true?

A You have a greater than even chance of picking a yellow marble.
　You have a less than even chance of picking a green marble.

B You have an even chance of picking a yellow marble.
　You have a greater than even chance of picking a red marble.

C You have a greater than even chance of picking a green marble.
　You have an even chance of picking a yellow marble.

D You are certain to pick a marble.
　You have a greater than even chance of picking a yellow marble.

E You have a less than even chance of picking a red marble.
　You have a less than even chance of picking a green marble.

Please turn over

44 A bag contains some coloured pencils. There are:

two black   three red   four blue   five green   six yellow

What is the probability that I don't pick a red?

A $\frac{17}{20}$ B $\frac{14}{17}$ C $\frac{3}{20}$ D $\frac{16}{19}$ E $\frac{6}{10}$

---

45 How is the time '9.45 in the evening' written in 24-hour clock notation?

A 21:45   B 19:45   C 09:45   D 17:45   E 22:45

---

46 Andrew goes to the library to return his six books. They are all overdue by one week so he has to pay six fines. He gets 16p in change from £1.

A 21p   B 14p   C £1   D £0.16   E 84p

---

47 The total attendance in one season for Nelson Football Club was 810 000. They played 27 games. What is the mean attendance for the season?

A 27 000   B 37 000   C 81 000   D 30 000   E 40 000

48

What is the approximate size of angle y marked on the trapezium above?

A 30°   B 45°   C 70°   D 90°   E 110°

---

49 The area of a rectangle is 36 cm². What could be the perimeter of the rectangle?

A 6 cm   B 9 cm   C 12 cm   D 18 cm   E 26 cm

---

50 How many hexagons are needed to make the next shape in this sequence?

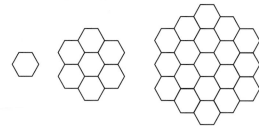

A 18   B 27   C 30   D 37   E 47

Bond N E W EDITION

11⁺ Test Papers

Maths

Multiple-choice Test 2

Read the following:

- Do not begin the test or open this booklet until told to do so.

- Work as quickly and as carefully as you can.

- Answers should be marked in pencil in the answer booklet provided, not in this test booklet.

- You may do rough working on a separate sheet of paper.

- If you make a mistake rub out the mistake and write the new answer clearly.

- Be careful to keep your place in the accompanying answer booklet.

- You will have 50 minutes to complete the test.

- Calculators should not be used.

Text © Andrew Baines 2007
Original illustrations © Nelson Thornes Ltd 2007

The right of Andrew Baines to be identified as author of this work has been asserted by him in accordance with the Copyright, Designs and Patents Act 1988.

First published in 2003 by:
Nelson Thornes Ltd

This edition published in 2007 by:
Nelson Thornes Ltd, Delta Place, 27 Bath Road
CHELTENHAM GL53 7TH, United Kingdom

07 08 09 10 11 / 10 9 8 7 6 5 4 3 2 1

A catalogue record for this book is available from the British Library

ISBN 978 0 7487 8482 0

Page make-up by Tech Set Ltd

Printed and bound in Croatia by Zrinski

Published by Nelson Thornes. Nelson Thornes is a Wolters Kluwer company, and is not associated in any way with NFER-Nelson.

1 A chef is preparing some cakes. Each cake needs seven eggs. How many whole cakes can be made with 144 eggs?

A   19   B   20   C   21   D   7   E   1008

2 67 890   The digit 8 in this number has a value of 800. What is the value of the digit 7?

A   70 000   B   7   C   700   D   67 000   E   7000

3

This scalene triangle has angles q, r and s marked.
Angle r is 49° and angle s is 37°.
What is the size of angle q?

NOT DRAWN TO SCALE

A   266°   B   86°   C   286°

D   270°   E   49°

4 Dev is drawing a plan of his garden. He is using a scale of 2 cm to 5 m. The driveway is 12.5 m long. How long should he draw the driveway on his plan?

A   12.5 m   B   2 cm   C   5 cm   D   2.5 cm   E   5.2 cm

5 Which answer has a different value to the others?

A $\frac{6}{8}$ of 100   B   75% of 100   C $\frac{3}{4}$ of 100   D   0.075 of 100   E $\frac{24}{32}$ of 100

6 A school sends a letter home to the parents/guardians of all 780 pupils in the school.
85% of the parents/guardians have replied in the first week.
What number have not replied in the first week?

A   673   B   117   C   850   D   127   E   663

7 Leela has been collecting football stickers for two years. Some cost her 10p and others cost her 5p. She has bought 56 of the more expensive stickers and 75 of the cheaper stickers. What is the total amount she has spent?

A   £5.60   B   £9.35   C   £10.30   D   £9.45   E   £3.75

8 Gavin spent twice as long on the Internet on Tuesday as he did on Wednesday. He then spent three times as long on Thursday as he did on Wednesday. On Friday he spent two hours longer than he did on Thursday. If he spent eight hours on the Internet on Friday, how long did he spend on Tuesday?

A   4 hours   B   2 hours   C   6 hours   D   3 hours 20 mins   E   8 hours

9 The school maths club started in 2005 with 23 pupils. In 2006 there were twice as many as in 2005. In 2007 there were twice as many as in 2006. How many pupils were in the maths club in 2007?

A   82   B   23   C   92   D   46   E   2007

10

What is the area of triangle DEF?

A   12.32 cm²   B   18.96 cm²   C   60 cm²

D   30 cm²   E   18 cm²

10 cm   6.32 cm   6 cm

D   6 cm   E

Continue to the next page

11 What is the missing number?

104	98	92
110	104	98
?	110	104

A 116   B 104   C 92

D 96   E 98

12 The pie chart shows proportions of number of doors on cars in a car park.
There are 60 cars in the car park.
How many cars have three doors?

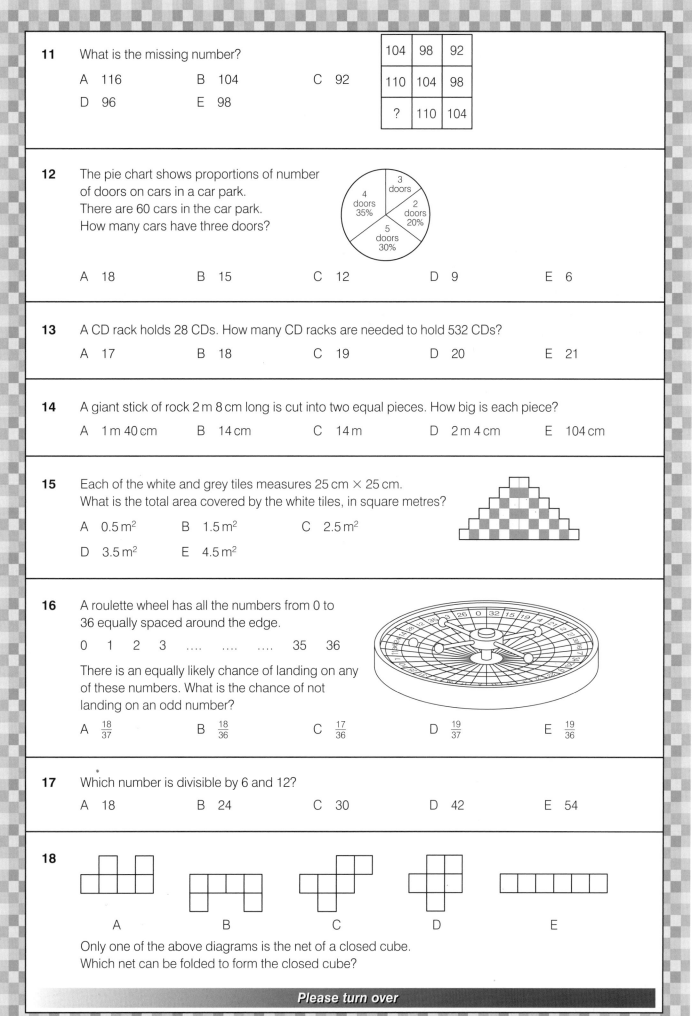

A 18   B 15   C 12   D 9   E 6

13 A CD rack holds 28 CDs. How many CD racks are needed to hold 532 CDs?

A 17   B 18   C 19   D 20   E 21

14 A giant stick of rock 2 m 8 cm long is cut into two equal pieces. How big is each piece?

A 1 m 40 cm   B 14 cm   C 14 m   D 2 m 4 cm   E 104 cm

15 Each of the white and grey tiles measures 25 cm × 25 cm.
What is the total area covered by the white tiles, in square metres?

A 0.5 m²   B 1.5 m²   C 2.5 m²

D 3.5 m²   E 4.5 m²

16 A roulette wheel has all the numbers from 0 to 36 equally spaced around the edge.

0   1   2   3   35   36

There is an equally likely chance of landing on any of these numbers. What is the chance of not landing on an odd number?

A $\frac{18}{37}$ B $\frac{18}{36}$ C $\frac{17}{36}$ D $\frac{19}{37}$ E $\frac{19}{36}$

17 Which number is divisible by 6 and 12?

A 18   B 24   C 30   D 42   E 54

18

A   B   C   D   E

Only one of the above diagrams is the net of a closed cube.
Which net can be folded to form the closed cube?

Please turn over

19 This machine doubes and then subtracts 7.

? ———▶ [   ] ———▶ 99

Which number has been put in?

A   46   B   92   C   107   D   53   E   53.5

20 Morag delivers papers seven days a week. She earns £x each weekday, and twice each weekday amount for each weekend day. How much does she earn for the whole week?

A   £$5x$ B   £$7x$ C   £$9x$ D   £$11x$ E   £$14x$

21   1   4   9   ...   is the beginning of the sequence of square numbers.
The difference between the first pair of square numbers is $4 - 1 = 3$ difference = 3
The difference between the second pair of square numbers is $9 - 4 = 5$ difference = 5
Continue the sequence and find which is the first difference between a pair of square numbers that is not a prime number.

A   7   B   8   C   9   D   10   E   11

22

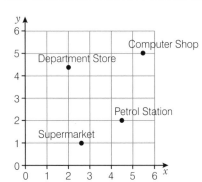

Write the coordinates of the Petrol Station.

A   (2, 4.5)

B   (2.5, 4.5)

C   (4.5, 2.5)

D   (4, 2)

E   (4.5, 2)

23 A skiing holiday costs £780 for each adult. There is a reduction of £150 for each child.
How much would it cost for Angus, his older sister who is nine years old, his mum and dad and his granny to go on holiday?

A   £3600   B   £2900   C   £2750   D   £3100   E   £2450

24 Look at these clouds of numbers.

14, 15, 16   15, 16, 18   16, 18, 20   15, 16, 24   14, 15, 20

   A   B   C   D   E

In which cloud are all the numbers multiples of either 4 or 5?

25 This bar chart shows the marks in a geography test. How many children scored fewer than 20 marks?

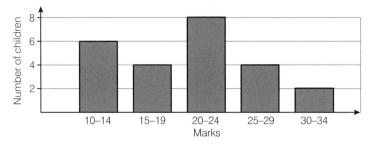

A   6

B   8

C   4

D   18

E   10

Continue to the next page

26 Which number which has the smallest value.

A 5.03 B 4.05 C 5.10 D 4.99 E 4.1

27 The subscription to join the 'Draw and Paint' evening class is £30.

Plus: £2.50 admin charge
£1.10 for HB pencils
£3.50 for pastels
£4.75 for brushes
£2.15 for water colours
£1.65 for paper.

What is the total cost?

A £46.55 B £45.65 C £16.65 D £46.60 E £30

28 Here is the plan of a room. What is the perimeter of the room?

A 37.5 m

B 36.5 m

C 24.5 m

D 32 m

E 37 m

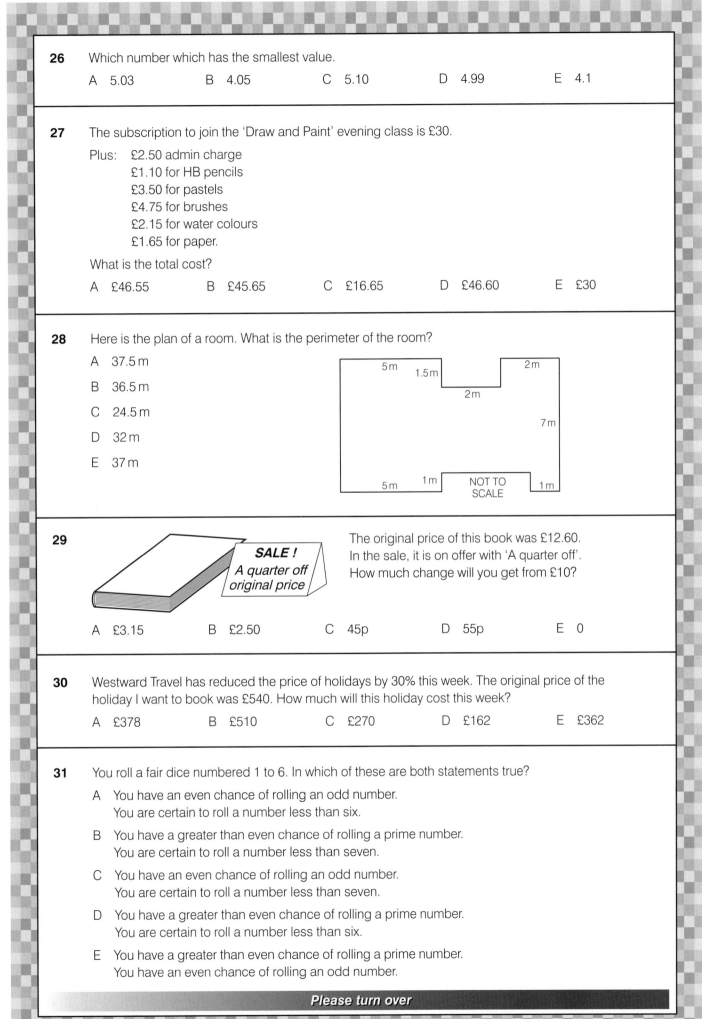

29 SALE !
A quarter off original price

The original price of this book was £12.60.
In the sale, it is on offer with 'A quarter off'.
How much change will you get from £10?

A £3.15 B £2.50 C 45p D 55p E 0

30 Westward Travel has reduced the price of holidays by 30% this week. The original price of the holiday I want to book was £540. How much will this holiday cost this week?

A £378 B £510 C £270 D £162 E £362

31 You roll a fair dice numbered 1 to 6. In which of these are both statements true?

A You have an even chance of rolling an odd number.
You are certain to roll a number less than six.

B You have a greater than even chance of rolling a prime number.
You are certain to roll a number less than seven.

C You have an even chance of rolling an odd number.
You are certain to roll a number less than seven.

D You have a greater than even chance of rolling a prime number.
You are certain to roll a number less than six.

E You have a greater than even chance of rolling a prime number.
You have an even chance of rolling an odd number.

Please turn over

5

32

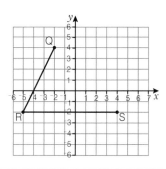

When point T is added to the diagram, QRST is a parallelogram.
What are the coordinates of the point T?

A (4, 4)   B (1, 4)

C (4, ⁻2)   D (7, 4)

E (6, 4)

---

33 Here is part of a conversion table for pounds (lb) to kilograms (kg) and kilograms to pounds.
Example: 5 pounds = 2.27 kg

	pounds to kg	kg to pounds
5	2.27 kg	11.02 lb
6	2.72 kg	?
7	3.18 kg	15.43 lb
8	3.63 kg	17.64 lb

Which figure is missing from the table?

A   11.44 lb   B   12.03 lb   C   13.10 lb   D   14.44 lb   E   13.23 lb

---

34 Tariq collected the following data during a survey of his year group.

	Favourite musical instrument		
	Drum	Recorder	Guitar
Boys	31	?	11
Girls	13	19	15

One hundred and ten pupils completed the survey. How many boys gave recorder as their favourite instrument?

A   29   B   99   C   39   D   18   E   21

35

A   B   C   D   E

One interior angle on each polygon has been marked.

Example: The interior angle of a square is 90°.

Which of the regular polygons above has the largest interior angle?

---

36 If: 5x + 9 = 54 − 4x what is x?

A   5   B   9   C   63   D   45   E   8

---

37 There are 520 pupils at Sporting School. 433 take part in events at the annual sports day.
How many pupils do not take part in the events?

A   77   B   87   C   97   D   433   E   93

---

38 Seb walks home from the supermarket carrying his shopping in two bags. They contain an average size chicken, a bag of sugar and a 500 g jar of coffee. What is most likely to be the approximate total weight of his shopping?

A   0.5 kg   B   1.5 kg   C   3.5 kg   D   6.5 kg   E   10.5 kg

Continue to the next page

39

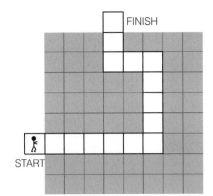

FINISH

START

Your task is to guide the robot along the white squares on the plan.

It starts on the square marked START and finishes on the square marked FINISH.

It can only move FORWARD, TURN RIGHT 90° and TURN LEFT 90°.

Which are the correct instructions?

A   FORWARD 6, TURN LEFT 90°, FORWARD 4, TURN LEFT 90°, FORWARD 2, TURN RIGHT 90°, FORWARD 3

B   FORWARD 6, TURN RIGHT 90°, FORWARD 5, TURN RIGHT 90°, FORWARD 2, TURN LEFT 90°, FORWARD 2

C   FORWARD 5, TURN RIGHT 90°, FORWARD 4, TURN LEFT 90°, FORWARD 2, TURN LEFT 90°, FORWARD 2

D   FORWARD 6, TURN LEFT 90°, FORWARD 5, TURN RIGHT 90°, FORWARD 2, TURN LEFT 90°, FORWARD 2

E   FORWARD 6, TURN LEFT 90°, FORWARD 4, TURN LEFT 90°, FORWARD 2, TURN RIGHT 90°, FORWARD 2

---

40   These are the wages of seven people in a company.

£100   £140   £110   £120   £130   £210   £425

What is the median wage?

A £133   B £425   C £100   D £130   E £120

---

41   Heather thinks that her mum is drinking too many cups of coffee a day.
Heather asks her mum some questions and completes this table.

Day	Mon	Tues	Wed	Thurs	Fri	Sat	Sun
Cups of coffee	5		6	4	5	3	9

Her mum says her mean is 6. How many cups did she drink on Tuesday?

A 6   B 5   C 10   D 15   E 0

---

42   Liam used this decision tree to sort a pile of discarded plastic and metal.

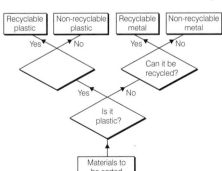

What is missing from the empty shape?

A   Recyclable

B   Non-recyclable

C   Can it be recycled?

D   Is it metal?

E   Is it non-recyclable?

Please turn over

43 Grace buys two computer games on holiday for €32 and €28. She calculates that one game costs £20 and the other costs £17.50. How much would a €4 adapter cost if her calculations are correct?

A £2.00   B £2.50   C £3.50   D £4.00   E £4.50

44 You start with a number. You multiply it by itself. Then multiply this number by the start number. The new number is 125. What is the value of the start number?

A 10   B 8   C 6   D 4   E 5

45

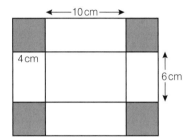

The shaded corners are cut out of this flat shape. It is then folded to make an open box.

What is the capacity of the box?

A 240 cm³

B 120 cm³

C 260 cm³

D 160 cm³

E 220 cm³

46 Deepak's street has 34 semi-detached houses and 16 detached houses. What fraction of the houses on the street are semi-detached?

A $\frac{34}{16}$ B $\frac{8}{17}$ C $\frac{18}{16}$ D $\frac{17}{25}$ E $\frac{50}{34}$

47 If you reflect this right-angled triangle in its dashed side you will make a quadrilateral.

What is the name of this quadrilateral?

A square   B rectangle   C rhombus   D parallelogram   E kite

48

The arrow shows how much the person weighs. The person is wearing a coat, which weighs 800 g. If they take it off and place it on the table, what would the new weight be?

A 30.2 kg   B 31.2 kg   C 29.2 kg   D 29.6 kg   E 29.8 kg

49 $5p - 7q + 3r = t$

If $p = 7$, $q = 4$, $r = 9$, what is the value of t?

A 20   B 90   C 36   D 24   E 34

50 Which of these words does not have a vertical line of symmetry?

A WOW   B TOT   C SOS   D MUM   E AXA

Bond NEW EDITION

11⁺ Test Papers

Maths

Multiple-choice Test 3

Read the following:

- Do not begin the test or open this booklet until told to do so.

- Work as quickly and as carefully as you can.

- Answers should be marked in pencil in the answer booklet provided, not in this test booklet.

- You may do rough working on a separate sheet of paper.

- If you make a mistake rub out the mistake and write the new answer clearly.

- Be careful to keep your place in the accompanying answer booklet.

- You will have 50 minutes to complete the test.

- Calculators should not be used.

Text © Andrew Baines 2007
Original illustrations © Nelson Thornes Ltd 2007

The right of Andrew Baines to be identified as author of this work has been asserted by him in accordance with the Copyright, Designs and Patents Act 1988.

All rights reserved. No part of this publication may be reproduced or transmitted in any form or by any means, electronic or mechanical, including photocopying, recording or any information storage and retrieval system, without permission in writing from the publisher or under licence from the Copyright Licensing Agency Ltd, of Saffron House, 6–10 Kirby Street, London, EC1N 8TS.

Any person who commits any unauthorised act in relation to this publication may be liable to criminal prosecution and civil claims for damages.

First published in 2003 by:
Nelson Thornes Ltd

This edition published in 2007 by:
Nelson Thornes Ltd, Delta Place, 27 Bath Road
CHELTENHAM GL53 7TH, United Kingdom

07 08 09 10 11 / 10 9 8 7 6 5 4 3 2 1

A catalogue record for this book is available from the British Library

ISBN 978 0 7487 8482 0

Page make-up by Tech Set Ltd

Printed and bound in Croatia by Zrinski

Published by Nelson Thornes. Nelson Thornes is a Wolters Kluwer company, and is not associated in any way with NFER-Nelson.

Nelson Thornes
a Wolters Kluwer business

1   If you halve Briony's mum's age and then add 4 the answer is 33. How old is Briony's mum?

     A   66   B   74   C   58   D   56   E   29

---

2   Last Saturday 90 families went into Horsforth Travel Shop. 24 families actually booked their holiday on that day. What proportion is this?

     A $\frac{1}{5}$ B $\frac{4}{15}$ C $\frac{1}{3}$ D $\frac{2}{9}$ E $\frac{1}{4}$

---

3 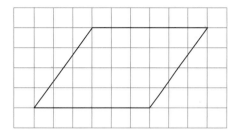

In this diagram, one small square represents $1\,\text{cm}^2$. What is the area of this shape?

A $20\,\text{cm}^2$

B $22\,\text{cm}^2$

C $24\,\text{cm}^2$

D $30\,\text{cm}^2$

E $32\,\text{cm}^2$

---

4   Which ratio is equivalent to the ratio $24:32$?

     A $12:30$ B $1:24$ C $6:9$ D $2:3$ E $3:4$

---

5   Joel used a decision tree to sort a tray of assorted chocolates. Each chocolate was either plain or milk chocolate coated. Some contained a nut, others did not. What is missing from the empty shape?

     A   Is it a milk chocolate?

     B   Does it contain a nut?

     C   Does it not contain a nut?

     D   Contains a nut

     E   Contains no nut

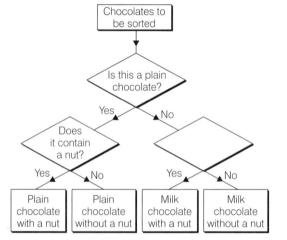

---

6 

The pie chart for Class 6C shows proportions of pupils with a certain number of brothers and sisters.
There are 32 pupils in Class 6C.
How many pupils have one brother or sister?

     A   25   B   24   C   10

     D   8   E   6

7

	14		→ 47
13		18	→ 47
19		?	→ 47

↓47   ↓47   ↓47

When every space in the grid is filled in, each row and each column adds up to 47. Which number should be in the square with the question mark?

     A   11   B   12   C   9   D   10   E   19

Continue to the next page

8 This table shows the hours of sunshine last summer.

Month	May	June	July	August	September
Hours	173	185	190	198	187

What is the range?

A 26   B 198   C 185   D 5   E 25

9

Four shapes have the same perimeter. Which shape has a different perimeter from the others?

---

10 Which answer is neither a square number nor a cube number?

A 25   B 27   C 45   D 49   E 64

11

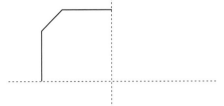

The diagram shows part of a shape and two lines of symmetry. What is the name of the complete shape?

A irregular quadrilateral

B irregular hexagon

C irregular octagon

D irregular decagon

E irregular dodecagon

---

12 In a nursery there are 13 boys and 16 girls. What fraction of the nursery is made up of boys?

A $\frac{1}{3}$ B $\frac{3}{6}$ C $\frac{13}{29}$ D $\frac{16}{29}$ E $\frac{4}{7}$

---

13 For which of these statements can you say that there is no chance of the event happening?

A It will snow next Christmas.   B I will grow taller than my mother.

C It will get dark tomorrow night.   D It will rain next month.

E I can pick a prime between 20 and 22.

14

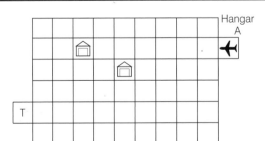

Your task is to guide the aeroplane from Hangar A to the terminal at T. It can only move FORWARD, TURN RIGHT 90° and TURN LEFT 90°. Which instructions will guide the plane to the terminal avoiding the other hangars?

A   FORWARD 6, TURN RIGHT 90°, FORWARD 2, TURN LEFT 90°, FORWARD 4

B   FORWARD 5, TURN LEFT 90°, FORWARD 3, TURN RIGHT 90°, FORWARD 5

C   FORWARD 6, TURN LEFT 90°, FORWARD 3, TURN RIGHT 90°, FORWARD 4

D   FORWARD 1, TURN RIGHT 90°, FORWARD 3, TURN RIGHT 90°, FORWARD 9

E   FORWARD 3, TURN LEFT 90°, FORWARD 2, TURN RIGHT 90°, FORWARD 4

Please turn over

15 What fraction of 3 hours is 15 minutes?

    A $\frac{3}{15}$ B $\frac{1}{4}$ C $\frac{1}{5}$ D $\frac{1}{12}$ E $\frac{1}{45}$

---

16 Li has swimming lessons three times a week for a 14-week period. Each lesson costs £3.20. What is the total cost of all the lessons?

    A £132.40   B 134.40   C £9.60   D £124.40   E £44.80

---

17 The area of the rectangle is 13 cm².

What is the area of the triangle?

    A 6.5 cm²   B 26 cm²   C 19.5 cm²

    D 7.5 cm²   E 5.5 cm²

---

18 Mira has drawn a plan of her school playing field. She uses a scale of 1 cm to 6 m. On the plan the long jump pit is 3 cm. What is the real length of the long jump pit?

    A 12 m   B 7 m   C 36 m   D 9 m   E 18 m

---

19 Which word has a horizontal line of symmetry?

    COX   NON   DAD   MUM   HIT

---

20 Jack does not like plain crisps. He surveys his 36 classmates to see if they agree. He asks: "Do you like plain crisps? Answer Yes or No." Three-quarters of them said "Yes". How many of his classmates said "No"?

    A 24   B 8   C 11   D 22   E 9

---

21 Samir has a pocket full of change. He decides to count it up to see how much he has. He has a two pound coin, three fifty pence pieces, seven five pence pieces and six one pence pieces. How much money does he have?

    A £3.81   B £3.85   C £2.91   D £3.91   E £4.06

---

22 Katrin's local card shop has 63 different types of birthday card. $\frac{3}{7}$ of them are for a boy's birthday. From how many cards can she choose for her friend Matthew?

    A 28   B 27   C 30   D 21   E 36

---

23 Which number which is exactly divisible by both 7 and 21.

    A 17   B 27   C 28   D 41   E 21

---

24 This is a net of a cuboid. It is then folded to make a box. What is the volume of the box?

    A 30 cm³   B 20 cm³   C 40 cm³

    D 35 cm³   E 50 cm³

5 cm 5 cm 3 cm 5 cm 5 cm 2 cm 3 cm 5 cm 5 cm 2 cm

Continue to the next page

25 Edward the elephant will be x years old in five years' time. How old was he four years ago?

    A $x - 4$ B $x + 9$ C $x - 9$ D $x - 1$ E $x + 1$

26 Circle the answer which has the largest value.

    A $\frac{3}{10}$ of 360   B 110   C 0.3 of 360   D $\frac{1}{3}$ of 360   E 30% of 360

27

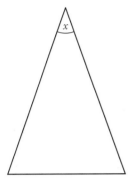

What is the approximate size of angle x marked on this isosceles triangle?

    A $10°$

    B $40°$

    C $70°$

    D $90°$

    E $140°$

28 A printing machine is set to print 700 copies of a book. Each book consists of 56 sheets of A3 paper. How many sheets of paper does the machine need to print all the books?

    A 39 200   B 70 000   C 49 200   D 33 600   E 36 200

29 This graph shows the favourite colours of Class 7AB.

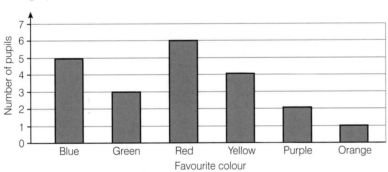

What is the modal colour?

    A Blue   B Green   C Red   D Purple   E Orange

30 Declan buys some stationery for £18.23. Because he is spending over £15 he gets a discount of £1.55. How much does he have to pay after his discount is taken into consideration?

    A £19.78   B £16.78   C £18.68   D £18.76   E £16.68

31 Kim's dad measures the length of his drive by counting strides. He counts 22 strides. There are four cars parked end-to-end up the drive. Kim writes down five different possible answers for the length of the drive. Which is correct?

    A 4 m   B 2000 mm   C 14 m   D 200 m   E 240 cm

32 How many matchsticks are needed to make the next shape in this sequence?

        A 16   B 32   C 38

    D 40   E 42

Please turn over

33 This machine multiplies by 5 and then divides by 3. Which number comes out?

21 ⟶ [ ] ⟶ ?

A 35   B 12.6   C 102
D 45   E 33

34 Thirty-one thousand five hundred and nine. Which answer shows this written as a number?

A 31 059   B 3159   C 3150.9   D 31 509   E 31 500.9

35 $f + 2g = 4h$ Which of the following is incorrect?

A $3f + 6g = 12h$ B $f + 2g - 4h = 0$ C $f = 4h - 2g$
D $0 = f + 2g - 4h$ E $2g = 4h + f$

36 There are 72 shops on the Eastward Town high street. $\frac{4}{9}$ of the shops on the high street sell some kind of food or drink. How many shops do not sell any kind of food or drink?

A 32   B 40   C 12   D 31   E 21

37 How many of the following shapes have at least two pairs of parallel sides?

Kite   Trapezium   Regular pentagon   Regular hexagon   Regular octagon
A 1   B 2   C 3   D 4   E 5

38 Look at this table showing the performance of the school Lacrosse team.

Year	Won	Drawn	Lost
2005	8	9	4
2006	12	6	3
2007	5	5	5

How many matches in total did the team not lose?

A 45   B 12   C 25   D 20   E 44

39 Karen and Pippa are both 150 cm tall and 12 years old. During the next four years Karen grows k centimetres per year and Pippa grows p centimetres per year. Pippa is taller.
When they are 16 years old how much taller is Pippa than Karen?

A $16(p - k)$ B $4(p - k) + 150$ C $p - k$ D $4(p - k)$ E $4(k - p)$

40

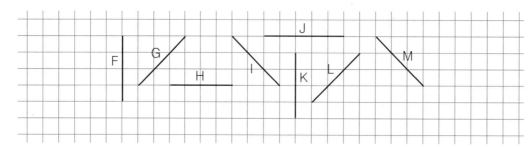

Which of these statements is correct?

A   Line F is parallel to line J.   B   Line G is perpendicular to line M.
C   Line H is a vertical line.   D   Line I is parallel to line L.
E   Line K is a horizontal line.

Continue to the next page

41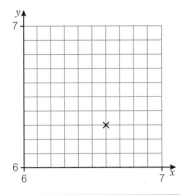

What are the coordinates of the cross.

A (6.3, 6.6)

B (6.6, 6.2)

C (6.7, 6.4)

D (6.7, 6.7)

E (6.6, 6.3)

42 Here is part of a conversion table for feet to metres and metres to feet.

Example: 5 feet = 1.53 m.

Which figure is missing from the table?

	feet to m	m to feet
5	1.53 m	?
6	1.83 m	19.68 ft
7	2.13 m	22.97 ft
8	2.44 m	26.25 ft

A 18.23 ft   B 19.01 ft   C 17.76 ft   D 15.33 ft   E 16.40 ft

43 6.996 143

What is this number to two decimal places?

A 7.00   B 6.9   C 6.99   D 6.9961   E 6.996

44

R   S   T   U   V

Which polygon has an interior reflex angle?

45 What are the coordinates of X, Y and Z?

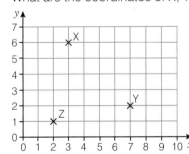

A X (3, 6)   Y (2, 7)   Z (1, 2)

B X (8, 3)   Y (7, 2)   Z (1, 2)

C X (3, 7)   Y (7, 3)   Z (2, 2)

D X (3, 6)   Y (7, 2)   Z (1, 2)

E X (3, 6)   Y (7, 2)   Z (2, 1)

46 Years 4 and 5 at Panto Primary School are performing a summer show. Year 4 has 62 children and Year 5 has 65 children. 73 children are acting. 48 children are working backstage. The rest are doing the front of house. How many are doing the front of house?

A 6   B 11   C 8   D 9   E 5

Please turn over

47   Thorne School did a survey on favourite crisp flavours.

Favourite flavour of crisps	
Plain	🍞🍞🍞
Salt and Vinegar	🍞🍞🍞
Cheese and Onion	🍞🍞
Bacon	🍞🍞
Prawn Cocktail	🍞🍞🍞🍞

Key: 🍞 stands for 8 children
            🍞 stands for 4 children

How many pupils liked Prawn Cocktail best?

A   16   B   20   C   24   D   28   E   32

---

48   There are 35 pupils in a class. $\frac{1}{7}$ travel to school by bus. $\frac{2}{7}$ travel to school by car.
The rest walk to school. How many pupils walk to school?

A   20   B   10   C   15   D   5   E   21

---

49   A milkwoman delivers milk to a housing estate. She does not want to visit the same street more than
once, but can pass over the same street corners. On which housing estate is this possible?

      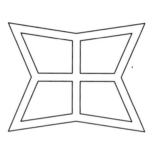      

A   B   C   D   E

---

50   Peter and Lauren were helping their grandad by carrying his shopping home for him.
Lauren was carrying a 440 g bag of potatoes and two bags of fruit each weighing 150 g.
The total weight of Peter's bags was exactly half the total weight of Lauren's bags.
How much weight did Peter carry?

A   590 g   B   370 g   C   315 g   D   360 g   E   470 g

Bond NEW EDITION

11+ Test Papers

Maths

Multiple-choice Test 4

Read the following:

- Do not begin the test or open this booklet until told to do so.

- Work as quickly and as carefully as you can.

- Answers should be marked in pencil in the answer booklet provided, not in this test booklet.

- You may do rough working on a separate sheet of paper.

- If you make a mistake rub out the mistake and write the new answer clearly.

- Be careful to keep your place in the accompanying answer booklet.

- You will have 50 minutes to complete the test.

- Calculators should not be used.

Text © Andrew Baines 2007
Original illustrations © Nelson Thornes Ltd 2007

The right of Andrew Baines to be identified as author of this work has been asserted by him in accordance with the Copyright, Designs and Patents Act 1988.

First published in 2003 by:
Nelson Thornes Ltd

This edition published in 2007 by:
Nelson Thornes Ltd, Delta Place, 27 Bath Road
CHELTENHAM GL53 7TH, United Kingdom

07 08 09 10 11 / 10 9 8 7 6 5 4 3 2 1

A catalogue record for this book is available from the British Library

ISBN 978 0 7487 8482 0

Page make-up by Tech Set Ltd

Printed and bound in Croatia by Zrinski

Published by Nelson Thornes. Nelson Thornes is a Wolters Kluwer company, and is not associated in any way with NFER-Nelson.

Nelson Thornes
a Wolters Kluwer business

1 There are 60 children at a Christmas Party, of whom 23 are boys. Approximately what proportion is this?

A $\frac{1}{2}$ B $\frac{1}{3}$ C $\frac{1}{4}$ D $\frac{2}{5}$ E $\frac{5}{12}$

2 What is the formula for the area of this shape?

A x^2 B y^2 C $4xy$

D $3xy$ E $(x + y)^2$

3 Ravi takes the bus from home to school then school to home for five days each week. Each fare is 57p. What is the total of the fares he pays each week?

A £5.80   B £5.70   C £4.70   D £2.85   E £5.60

4 350 pupils were asked how they came to school. The results are displayed in the pie chart. How many pupils came to school by car?

A 147   B 42   C 210

D 140   E 150

5 A joiner is building 14 cupboards in a new kitchen. Each cupboard requires 26 screws. How many screws will be required in total?

A 260   B 380   C 364   D 366   E 370

6 This machine divides by 4 and then multiplies by 5. Which number comes out?

92 ⟶ [   ] ⟶ ?

A 23   B 18.4   C 73.6
D 110   E 115

7 What percentage of the diagram has been shaded?

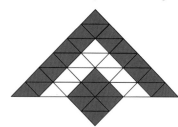

A 70%   B 65%

C 60%   D 40%

E 30%

8 Carmel has joined her local gym. She pays x pounds each month in membership fees. She also joins a Pilates class once a week and goes every week in the year. Each class costs y pounds. What is the total amount Carmel pays each year?

A $12x + y$ B $52(x + y)$ C $12x + 52y$ D $12(x + y)$ E $52x + 12y$

Continue to the next page

9 The Science Department is going on a day trip to the National Science Museum.
The trip costs £25 and 43 people are going and have paid the full amount.
How much money has been collected in total?

A £1000   B £1075   C £2150   D £1100   E £1125

10 There are 240 books in the school library. $\frac{1}{5}$ of the books are fiction. $\frac{2}{5}$ of the books are non-fiction.
The rest are reference books. How many reference books are in the school library?

A 72   B 96   C 144   D 98   E 94

11

	?	6	→ 33
9		13	→ 33
	10		→ 33

↓ 33   ↓ 33   ↓ 33

When every space in the grid is filled in, each row and
each column adds up to 33.
Which number should be in the square with the question mark?

A 6   B 9   C 11   D 12   E 13

12 A computer checks e-mails and news updates on a regular basis. The computer checks
e-mails every five minutes and news updates every seven minutes.
Neither work when both checks are being done at the same time and this causes an error
message on the screen. There is one error message after an hour and three error messages
after two hours. How many error messages are there after 5 hours?

A 6   B 7   C 8   D 9   E 10

13 Debbie wants to create her own small flower garden. She goes to the garden centre with her
mum and buys some bulbs. She buys:

5 bulbs at £1.20.   4 bulbs at 95p.   3 bulbs at 75p.   6 bulbs at 50p.   2 bulbs at £1.40.

How much is her total bill?

A £4.80   B £14.85   C £17.85   D £20.00   E £32.80

14 This table shows the results for Tanvi's favourite netball team.

Year	Won	Drawn	Lost
2005	9	3	1
2006	6	2	5
2007	5	8	0

How many matches in total did the team not win?

A 19   B 6   C 13   D 20   E 18

15 There are 500 sheets of paper in a ream. How many sheets of paper are in 6.5 reams?

A 3500   B 3000   C 3150   D 6500   E 3250

Please turn over

16 Woodside School did a survey on favourite fruit. Which of the numbers given below is the number of pupils who liked apples best?

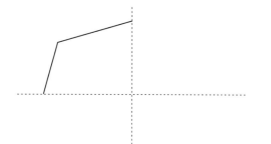

Favourite fruit	
Apple	⌒ ⌒
Orange	⌒ ⌒
Banana	
Pear	⌒ ⌒ ⌒ ⌒
Kiwi	⌒

Key: ⌒ stands for 6 children
⌒ stands for fewer than 6 children

A   6   B   12   C   18

D   0   E   11

17

The diagram shows part of a shape and two lines of symmetry. What is the name of the complete shape?

A   irregular quadrilateral

B   irregular hexagon

C   irregular octagon

D   irregular decagon

E   regular octagon

18 A map of the Yorkshire Dales is drawn to a scale of 1:25 000. What real distance does 1 cm on the map represent?

A   25 km   B   0.025 km   C   0.25 km   D   250 km   E   2.5 km

19 What does the digit 8 in 203 081 represent?

A   8   B   80   C   8000   D   800 000   E   800

20 Which container will hold about 0.5 litres when full?

A   a bath   B   a sink   C   a kettle   D   a milk bottle   E   an egg cup

21 Josh is going on a holiday for a week this August. He has paid a deposit of £50 towards the total cost of £225. He can afford to save £35 per month towards the total cost. How many months will it take him to save enough to pay the rest of the money?

A   4   B   5   C   6   D   7   E   8

22 The perimeter of a rectangle is 22 cm. If the lengths of two sides are both 10 cm, what is the area of the rectangle?

A   10 cm²   B   11 cm²   C   20 cm²   D   32 cm²   E   220 cm²

23

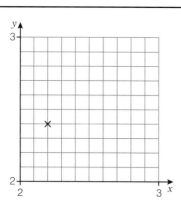

What are the coordinates of the cross?

A   (2.2, 2.4)

B   (2.1, 2.5)

C   (2.2, 2.3)

D   (2.1, 2.4)

E   (2.4, 2.2)

Continue to the next page

24

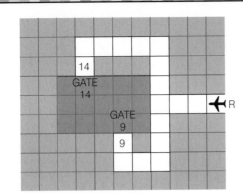

Your task is to guide the aeroplane from the Runway R to GATE 9.
It can only move FORWARD, TURN RIGHT 90° and TURN LEFT 90°.
Which instructions will guide the plane to the correct gate?

A   FORWARD 3, TURN RIGHT 90°, FORWARD 3, TURN LEFT 90°, FORWARD 2,
TURN RIGHT 90°, FORWARD 1

B   FORWARD 3, TURN LEFT 90°, FORWARD 3, TURN RIGHT 90°, FORWARD 2,
TURN LEFT 90°, FORWARD 1

C   FORWARD 3, TURN RIGHT 90°, FORWARD 3, TURN RIGHT 90°, FORWARD 2,
TURN RIGHT 90°, FORWARD 1

D   FORWARD 3, TURN LEFT 90°, FORWARD 3, TURN LEFT 90°, FORWARD 2,
TURN RIGHT 90°, FORWARD 1

E   FORWARD 3, TURN LEFT 90°, FORWARD 3, TURN RIGHT 90°, FORWARD 2,
TURN RIGHT 90°, FORWARD 1

---

25   Mr McCaskill is 6 feet 3 inches tall. Which is the closest to his height in metres?

A   1.8 m   B   1.9 m   C   2.0 m   D   2.1 m   E   2.2 m

---

26   400 g of a 2.2 kg bag of muesli is oats. What fraction of the bag is oats?

A $\frac{1}{9}$ B $\frac{1}{10}$ C $\frac{2}{11}$ D $\frac{3}{12}$ E $\frac{4}{26}$

---

27   What is the perimeter of this shape?

A $2a + 2b + 2c + 2d + 2e$

B $2a + 2b + 2c + 2d$

C $2a + b + c + 2d + 9e$

D $abcde$

E $abcd$

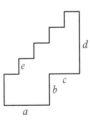

---

28   Which of these makes a word when rotated through 180°?

NOZE   NOS   HOSE   ICON   TON

---

29   Nankunda was x years old six years ago. How old will she be in seven years' time in terms of x?

A $x + 13$ B $x + 7$ C $x + 6$ D $x + 1$ E $x - 1$

---

30   Which number is both a square number and a cube number?

A   4   B   8   C   27   D   36   E   64

Please turn over

31 Which of these statements is incorrect?

A   Line P is parallel to line T.

B   Line R is perpendicular to line U.

C   Line T is a vertical line.

D   Line S is parallel to line V.

E   Line W is a horizontal line.

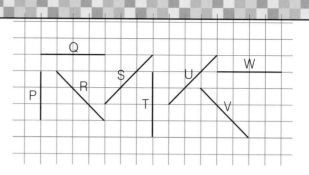

32

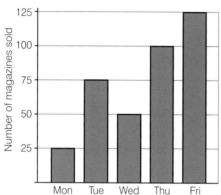

This shows the number of magazines sold by a shop in five days. How many more magazines were sold on Wednesday than on Monday?

A   25   B   50

C   75   D   100

E   125

33 Which one of these has the closest value to 1?

A   0.95   B   94.3%   C $\frac{24}{25}$ D   94.29%   E $\frac{24}{27}$

34 These are the temperatures in °C recorded at midday during Susan's two-week holiday.

26   28   27   28   26   25   26
25   27   28   29   31   31   28

What is the modal temperature?

A   28°C   B   27°C   C   31°C   D   30°C   E   29°C

35

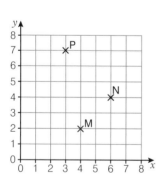

What are the coordinates of M, N and P?

A   M (4, 2)   N (4, 6)   P (4, 7)

B   M (4, 2)   N (6, 4)   P (3, 7)

C   M (4, 2)   N (7, 4)   P (7, 3)

D   M (2, 4)   N (6, 4)   P (3, 7)

E   M (5, 2)   N (6, 3)   P (3, 7)

36 Which ratio is not equivalent to the ratio 36:20?

A   18:10   B   9:5   C   27:15   D   54:30   E   46:25

37 David is three times as old as his sister. In two years' time he will be 14. How old is his sister?

A   3   B   12   C   4   D   16   E   5

Continue to the next page

38 A paperboy delivers papers to a housing estate. He does not want to visit the same street more than once, but can pass over the same street corners. On which housing estate is this possible?

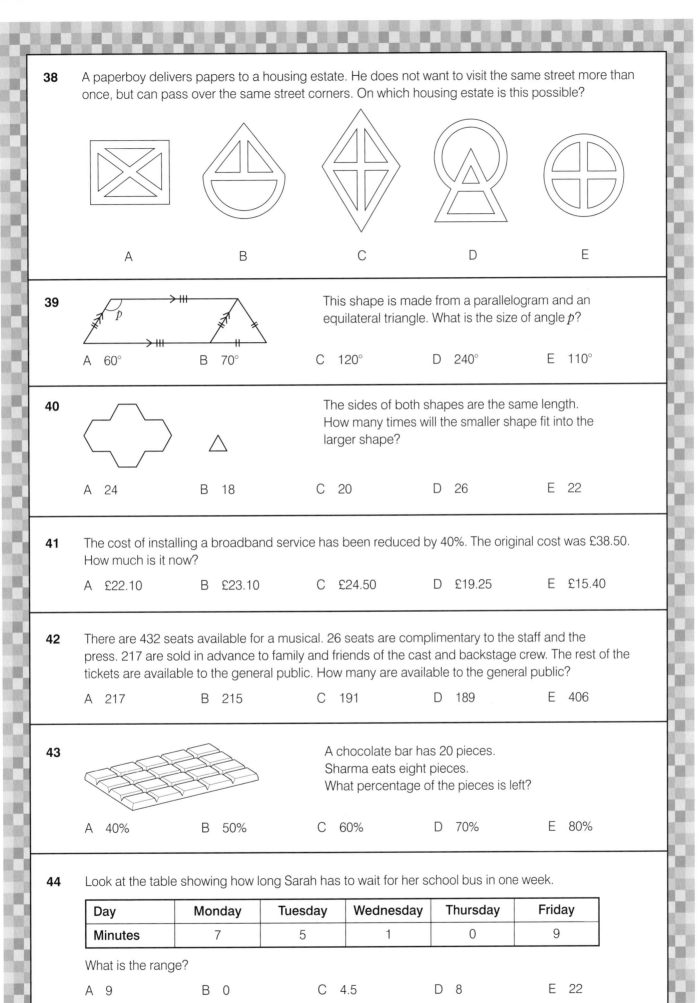

A   B   C   D   E

39 This shape is made from a parallelogram and an equilateral triangle. What is the size of angle p?

A 60°   B 70°   C 120°   D 240°   E 110°

40 The sides of both shapes are the same length. How many times will the smaller shape fit into the larger shape?

A 24   B 18   C 20   D 26   E 22

41 The cost of installing a broadband service has been reduced by 40%. The original cost was £38.50. How much is it now?

A £22.10   B £23.10   C £24.50   D £19.25   E £15.40

42 There are 432 seats available for a musical. 26 seats are complimentary to the staff and the press. 217 are sold in advance to family and friends of the cast and backstage crew. The rest of the tickets are available to the general public. How many are available to the general public?

A 217   B 215   C 191   D 189   E 406

43 A chocolate bar has 20 pieces.
Sharma eats eight pieces.
What percentage of the pieces is left?

A 40%   B 50%   C 60%   D 70%   E 80%

44 Look at the table showing how long Sarah has to wait for her school bus in one week.

Day	Monday	Tuesday	Wednesday	Thursday	Friday
Minutes	7	5	1	0	9

What is the range?

A 9   B 0   C 4.5   D 8   E 22

Please turn over

45

 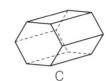

A   B   C   D   E

Which of these solids has an even number of edges and an odd number of faces?

46 The coordinates of the end points of five lines are given below. Which line is perpendicular to the line in the diagram?

A   (2, 1) and (3, 4)   B   (1, 4) and (4, 4)

C   (1, 1) and (4, 4)   D   (1, 4) and (4, 1)

E   (1, 2) and (3, 1)

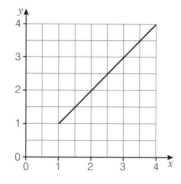

47 A thermometer shows the temperature at midday and midnight outside the school office. On Wednesday it showed the following:

Midday	8°C
Midnight	⁻3°C

What is the difference between these two temperatures in degrees Celsius?

A   5°C   B   3°C   C   8°C   D   12°C   E   11°C

48 Rulers cost the same as erasers. Four of the following cost the same. Which does not cost the same as the rest?

A   two rulers, three erasers

B   one eraser, one ruler, six pencils

C   two erasers, two rulers, two pencils

D   two rulers, two erasers, four pencils

E   three erasers, one ruler, two pencils

49 Which number has the value closest to 7?

A   7.001   B   6.989   C   7.101   D   6.99   E   7.0

50 This bar chart shows the times of goals scored in school football matches in one season. How many goals were scored after more than 45 minutes had passed?

A   7   B   16

C   15   D   32

E   8

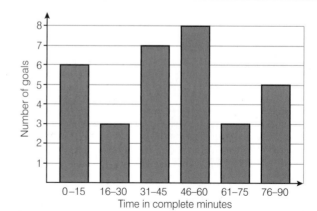